YOUR TOP

INVESTING

MOVES FOR

RETIREMENT

◆ **JUNIUS ELLIS**
Wall Street Columnist
AND THE EDITORS OF MONEY

MONEY BOOKS ◆ Time Inc. Home Entertainment / 1271 Avenue of the Americas / New York, NY 10020

MONEY MAGAZINE

TIME INC. HOME ENTERTAINMENT

MONEY BOOK SERIES

CONTENTS

4 ◆ MANAGE YOUR MONEY LIKE A PRO 87

5 ◆ REDUCE YOUR FUND PORTFOLIO'S RISK 135

6 ◆ GROW AND GUARD YOUR 401(K) MONEY 149

INDEX 175

1

YOU CAN

RETIRE A

MILLIONAIRE

*T*ake a moment please to ponder the following statement. You have a good shot at reaching retirement with assets exceeding $1 million if you start saving and investing now. That's right, $1 million. Here's the math. Let's say you are 40, with a household income of $84,000, the median for MONEY subscribers. Let's also assume that you want to retire on an inflation-adjusted 80% of your current income; that you will put 10% of your salary every year into a 401(k) retirement account with a fairly typical 50% in matching funds from your employer; and that you might earn 10% on your money (a little below the stock market's average over the past 60 years). In this scenario, you would hit age 65 with $1.7 million in your account even if you are starting from zero today.

Let's be realistic, of course. By the time today's 40-year-olds retire, inflation will have made a million dollars a somewhat less awesome figure than it is today. Even so, it will never be chump change. And you will inevitably face obstacles on the way to becoming a millionaire. If you are just starting out, you may find that your beginner's salary leaves you barely enough to cope with student loans, let alone max out on your 401(k) contribution. If you're married with kids, you will have to find some way to finesse college expenses that loom just one step ahead of your own retirement bills. And at any age, you can fall victim to an asset-crushing setback such as divorce.

Still, at every stage of your life, you can control your retirement prospects depending on how much you save and when you save it or how aggressively you invest and when you plan to retire. Even if you are 50 years old, in the earlier example, without a penny saved, you could still hit retirement with a million in the bank by cranking your savings up to 15% of your salary and staying on the job two years longer than you had planned. And remember that you have help. In addition to Social Security, the government gives you tax breaks when you save in retirement plans like 401(k)s and IRAs. Chances are, your employer is willing to lend a hand. Some 90% of large and midsize companies offer 401(k) plans, and 80% of these employers usually match 50% of whatever you save up to 6% of your salary. But 401(k) plans are not exempt from problems, as we explain in Chapter 6. Many employers, for example, undercut their plan's benefits by allowing the 401(k) to overcharge employees.

This book can help you reach your goal. In this chapter, we profile typical individuals and couples who face some of the same obstacles that you will encounter on the path to a bountiful retirement.

◆ A Young Single Needs Patience

When she isn't playing alto sax or teaching music to school children, Laura Griesemer, 26, of Middlebury, Vt. is something of a magician. With an ease that amazes even Griesemer, she can make her $1,450 a month take-home pay disappear. "I don't know where the money goes," she says, a lament that most twentysomethings and their parents find all too familiar. The leaks in her cash flow are about what you'd expect from someone just getting a start on life. These include a $230 share of the monthly mortgage payment on the two-bedroom condo she and her boyfriend Scott Barbieri, 26, bought last year; another $380 in car payments; and $140 for gas and insurance combined. Although she earned an extra $4,200 last year giving music lessons, this money also vanished into closing costs on the condo and other housing expenses. That's not an auspicious start for a millionaire in the making.

Like most people her age, Griesemer finds it hard to sacrifice for a financial goal three or four decades in the future. She socked away only $1,000 of her $24,700 salary last year in Vermont's retirement savings plan for teachers, at a return of about 5%. She'll be vested in nine years. Meanwhile, she also has $2,800 earning the same dismal return in a pension plan from a former teaching job. But at least she understands what is at stake. "I realize that saving early gives you a lot more money in the end than saving late," Laura says. "So I want to put away as much as I possibly can." And she'll have more to salt away later this year when her salary rises to $27,900 thanks to her new master's degree.

Start saving as much as you can. If a 26–year–old like Laura puts $2,000 a year into a tax–deferred savings plan earning 10% a year, he or she will have $803,000 by age 65. But most of it will come from the compounding on the early savings. Even if Laura socks away $2,000 a year for only 10 years and then stops, the nest egg will total $506,000 at age 65, far more than the $297,000 she would have if she didn't start saving until age 36 but continued steadily to age 65. The ideal vehicles for the ride to the $1 million mark are retirement plans like 401(k)s. Laura qualifies to contribute to a 403(b) plan where she works, a relative of the 401(k) offered to employees of nonprofits. In either plan, every dollar you save effectively counts as a tax deduction in the year you take it. Let's assume you're in the 28% tax bracket. To save a dollar you actually give up only 72¢ in after–tax take–home pay. So MONEY urged Laura to save the maximum permitted by her plan, or 20% of her pay.

When it comes to choosing investments, figure on putting at least 75% of your savings into your plan's stock funds. Then do your best to ignore market fluctuations. A 26–year–old has plenty of time to recover from a market slide or two or three. If Laura does that, she may be able to mimic the market's long–term return of just under 11% annually. In that case, assuming she keeps working for the next 29 years, she could retire a 55–year–old millionaire.

◆ A COUPLE ALSO SAVES FOR THE KIDS

Vickie and Kevin Jones, 44 and 36, of Fremont, Calif. have two incomes, 401(k) plans, pensions and children. Parents of Jade, 5, and Chauncey, 9 months, they also have two sets of college bills to face before they can retire. Like many baby boomers who have produced 50% more children after age 30 than the previous generation, the Joneses began building their family later in life than their parents did. That means they will be slogging through college expenses in their mid–fifties, just when they should begin their savings sprint toward retirement.

For all parents, trying to squeeze out money to amass a college fund while salting something away for the future empty nest is like asking the same dollar to do two jobs. Vickie and Kevin Jones have made the task more difficult by setting their sights high. When they think about the future, they envision a big–ticket Stanford University education for both of their kids and a retirement in which they live as well or even better than they do now in pricey northern California.

That will be tough for the two employees of Bank of America, where Kevin works as an unemployment insurance administrator and Vickie is an administrative assistant. We figure they should aim for an inflation-adjusted retirement income of $57,600 to maintain their standard of living. To hit that target, the couple would need assets of $1.8 million, a long reach from the $61,000 they have today. That cache is divided between two Bank of America pension plans and two 401(k)s. Kevin puts 5% of his $37,000 pretax salary into his 401(k), and the company matches his contributions a generous dollar for dollar. Vickie contributes 3% of her $35,000 and gets a dollar-for-dollar match too.

Finance your retirement first. At the Joneses' current rate of saving, their retirement accounts will total around $906,000 by the time Vickie turns 65. And that's without counting the tuition at Stanford, which will cost $75,000 a year by the time Jade is a freshman. Thus Kevin and Vickie must raise their savings by $2,860 a year, which may mean pushing hard for big salary increases. And they must earn one percentage point a year more on their investments, which will require more aggressive investing. Fortunately, they have no plans to retire early. In fact, with an eight-year age difference, Kevin will be working for quite a while after Vickie retires.

It usually makes sense to review your investments to see whether you can squeeze higher returns out of your portfolio. Judging from the way 401(k) participants overall divide their money, many investors have plenty of room for improvement. Employees often rely far too heavily on safe but low-returning investments and tend to keep too much money in their firm's stock.

The Joneses are guilty of both errors. About half of their retirement portfolio is invested in Bank of America stock and 40% is in fixed-income securities. The rest is in a blue-chip growth fund. We noted that the Joneses could probably boost their returns from 9% to 10% a year without any increase in risk by moving at least half of their Bank of America stock and half of their fixed-income funds into their 401(k)'s growth funds. To achieve similar returns with even less risk, we advised them to put all but 10% of their company's stock in the growth funds.

Coming up with any extra cash to save is more difficult. Says Kevin: "With a mortgage and two kids in daycare, it's an expensive life." So it's important for the couple to concentrate their saving where they'll get the highest payoff. That's their 401(k) plan, with its handsome dollar-for-dollar match. Vickie needs to save at least 5% of her income, not 3%. By scraping up that extra $700 a year, she'll get another $700 a year from her employer. Even if your 401(k) matches a more conventional 50%, that still amounts to a guaranteed 50% return. No other investment comes close. We also suggested the couple try to find ways to put still more of their pay into their 401(k). Any amount beyond what's permitted by their employer has to come out of after-tax salary and there's no match. But the money will still grow tax deferred, making it a better investment option than an alternative that's taxed every year.

As for saving for both college and retirement, the wisest course is to concentrate first on your own future. By the time your children are college bound, they may be eligible for loans or scholarships that are impossible to foresee today. You can demand that your kids pay some of their own way for college. But there's not much chance that your children will fund your retirement.

◆ A DIVORCING DAD MUST START OVER

With a marital split in his near future, Thomas Milligan, 46, figures his assault on $1 million will have to wait. Though the Corpus Christi pathologist earns $110,000 a year and another $50,000 in lecture and consulting fees, his assets total just $143,000. He'll likely wind up with less than half that amount when his 18-year marriage ends soon. Divorce often has a devastating effect on people's retirement planning. While divorced moms usually fare worse than dads, both sexes must start over with less money and less time to build assets.

Right now, Milligan is focusing his attention on his two boys, ages seven and eight. "I want to make sure I can do more for them than my parents could do for me," he says. But it's time Milligan concentrated on his own future. He will need a retirement income of $128,000 in today's dollars to maintain his standard of living. To pull that off, he would need to acquire a sum of $3.3 million by the time he retires at age 65. His $127,000 retirement portfolio consists of two 403(b) plans from former employers–one managed by the insurance and pension giant TIAA-CREF and the other with insurer USAA. He also owns a $16,000 variable annuity that he bought from USAA. The divorce will have a blistering effect on his investment portfolio, however. Milligan expects to wind up with about 40% of the assets that he has today.

Go for growth to recover lost ground. Most of his retirement money is now riding on full-throttle growth stocks. "College is at least a decade off for my kids and I don't plan to retire before 65," says Milligan. "So I don't worry much about short-term risk." We estimate that his current retirement portfolio will be worth roughly $350,000 at 65, assuming an average return of 10% annually. And if he socks away another $2,400 a month in stocks, or 18% of his income, he could add $1,750,000 to his retirement stash over 19 years. Milligan thinks he can swing this. In addition, if he maxes out at $9,500 annually on a new 403(b) plan that will go into effect later this year, he could add as much as $1.2 million to his savings. That could make for a pretty rosy retirement.

Milligan's high-risk stock portfolio, however, relies entirely on U.S. funds. Putting 15% of his money in international stock funds could give him returns that are comparable to an all-America portfolio without any increase in risk. When it comes to college bills for the boys, we again invoke our advice of saving for yourself first. Since Milligan will still be working when his kids are through college, he can probably pay their tuition as they go, from his earnings and savings. When the boys get older, he can help them buy their first homes with some of the cash in his retirement war chest. But, first, he has to build that war chest.

◆ BUSINESS PARTNERS PLAN THEIR EXIT

Joel Goobich and his wife Bonnie have put everything into their business and expect their business to do the same for them someday. "I'm not calling it retirement," says Joel, 41. "But I want to cash out as a millionaire." Five and a half years ago, with $15,000 seed money from their home equity, the couple started Colorations, which makes arts-and-crafts materials for kids. Today their Duluth, Ga. company has six full-time employees and sales of $1 million annually. The Goobiches plan to sell out in five years.

Joel develops products and manages sales while Bonnie, 38, runs the office. They have plowed most of what they have earned back into the company. This year they are paying themselves a $100,000 salary. Aside from the business, the couple's other investments are a pair of IRAs,

PLAN	AVAILABLE TO	BEST FOR	MAXIMUM CONTRIBUTION
401(k)[7]	Employees of for-profit businesses	Everyone who qualifies	15% of salary, up to roughly $9,500[1]
403(b)	Employees of nonprofit organizations	Everyone who qualifies	20% of gross salary or $9,500, whichever is less
IRA[7]	Anyone with earned income	Those who don't have company pension plans or who have put the maximum into their company plans	100% of wages up to $2,000; $2,250 if joint with spouse
SEP	The self-employed and employees of small businesses	Self-employed person who is a sole proprietor	13% of net self-employment income, or $22,500, whichever is less[2]
PROFIT-SHARING KEOGH	The self-employed and employees of unincorporated small businesses	Small-business owner who is funding a plan for himself and employees	Same as SEP[2]
MONEY-PURCHASE KEOGH	Same as profit-sharing Keogh	Small-business owner who wants to shelter more than allowed by profit-sharing Keogh	20% of net self-employment income, or $30,000, whichever is less[2]
VARIABLE ANNUITY	Anyone	Someone who has put the maximum into other plans and won't need the money for 10 years	None
FIXED ANNUITY	Anyone	Someone who has put the maximum into other plans and shuns risk	None

Notes: [1]Amount increases yearly with inflation rate. [2]Small-business owners fund the SEPs and Keoghs of their employees. [3]Percentage of employee's contribution [4]Some plans charge $20 to $30 annual administrative fees. [5]Surrender charges last six to eight years and typically decline by 1% a year. [6]All plans are subject to 10% income tax penalty, except in case of death or disability. [7]Effective this year, firms with

TAX BREAK ON CONTRIBUTIONS/ EARNINGS	MATCHING CONTRIBUTIONS	CHARGES/FEES	EARLY WITHDRAWAL[6]	NUMBER OF INVESTMENT OPTIONS
Yes/Yes	Anywhere from 0% to 100%,[3] but typically only up to 6% of salary	Depends on plan/annual expenses of 1% to 1.5% of assets[4]	Only in case of hardship	Three to 10, typically, depending on your employer's plan
Yes/Yes	Generally not available	Depends on plan/annual expenses of 1% to 3% of assets	Only in case of hardship and employee contributions only	One to 10, typically, depending on your employer's plan
Sometimes/Yes	None	Depends on investment/ zero to $50 annual fee	Always permitted	Nearly everything except real estate, collectibles and other hard assets
Yes/Yes	None	Depends on investment/ $10 to $30 a year	Always permitted	Same as IRA
Yes/Yes	None	Depends on investment/ up to $2,000 in annual administrative expenses	Always permitted	Unlimited
Yes/Yes	None	Same as profit-sharing Keogh	Always permitted	Unlimited
No/Yes	None	6% to 8% surrender charges[5]/annual expenses of 2% to 2.2% of assets	Always permitted	Anywhere from one to 22, but typically nine
No/Yes	None	Surrender charges of 6% to 8%[5]	Always permitted	One

100 or fewer employees can offer Simple 401(k)s or Simple IRAs that aim to reduce the administrative costs of retirement plans. The employer must make an annual contribution dollar for dollar of 2% of all eligible workers' pay or match employee contributions up to 3% of his or her salary, up to $4,800 for a Simple 401(k) and $6,000 for a Simple IRA. In both plans, workers can contribute up to $6,000 a year tax-deferred.

worth a total of about $43,000, invested in a hodgepodge of securities. Although the couple's two daughters, Dalit, 12, and Sivan, 9, are inching toward college age, the Goobiches have almost no tuition savings. "I hope the sale of the company will take care of that," says Joel.

If the company continues to grow at its present blistering 60% annual rate, sales will reach nearly $11 million in just five years. For that to happen, though, Joel will almost certainly need to raise capital for expansion by taking in a partner, complicating his ability to sell the business and reducing his share of the sale price. And this scenario depends on a lucrative buyout market over the next few years, an uncertain prospect. If the Goobiches don't find a willing investor, growth may be slower than expected. What's more, yearly sales may not be a reliable indicator of a company's future selling price. "It's hard to predict what competition, technology or even market conditions might bring down the road," says Frederick Lipman, author of the guide *How Much Is Your Business Worth?* "And there is no guarantee that a qualified buyer could be found, whatever the price."

Don't head for the exits too soon. As a retirement investment, a small business is the very definition of a high-risk, high-reward bet. On the other hand, a successful venture can be the shortest route between here and a seven-figure retirement. Consider that four of the top five people on the Forbes 400 list of the richest people in the U.S. built their fortunes through their own businesses. Still, entrepreneurs need to stay the course long enough to create real value for a potential acquirer or investor. What's more, the business itself can be a vehicle for the owners to build their retirement savings and even fund college for their kids. That's why we urged the Goobiches to stick with their company another 10 years.

Fortunately for Bonnie and Joel, entrepreneurs can choose among a handful of tax-deferred retirement plans designed for small businesses. The best option for the Goobiches is the SEP (simplified employee pension). It will let the couple shelter 15% of their eligible income a year, which in their case works out to about $12,250. Tax law requires you to fund SEP accounts for any employees who have worked for you during three of the past five years. But that provision rewards long-term employees and can help you keep experienced workers. So it usually justifies the cost. To buffer the riskiness of using their business as a main retirement vehicle, the couple should invest their SEPs in growth and income stock funds in hopes of earning at least 8% annually. To educate their children, the Goobiches can use a tax-saving strategem that's not available to families who work for other employers. They can hire the girls. Since Dalit and Sivan already work in product development, their parents can pay them a fair market wage and write it off. "They play with the paints and tell us how kids like them," says Bonnie. The Goobiches can deduct the girls' income as a payroll expense and then put the money they save in a college fund.

To maintain their current lifestyle in retirement, the Goobiches will need a retirement income of approximately $80,000 a year in today's dollars. If the business keeps growing, that goal should not present a big problem. Let's say that the company brings in annual sales of more than $8 million by the time they are 51 and 48. Let's also assume that the Goobiches then sell Colorations and walk away with an estimated $1.6 million. Meanwhile, if they have funded their SEPs for 10 years, those accounts could kick in another $214,000. Their IRA accounts might contribute $92,000 more, bringing their total retirement pot to around $1.9 million. That's a just reward for taking the risks of starting a business as well as a solid example of why it pays to aim high when contemplating your retirement.

◆ AVOID THESE RETIREMENT BLUNDERS

No matter how much you plan in advance, one big mistake can turn your retirement dream into a time of anxiety or even deprivation. For example, many retirees are so eager to wring more income out of their nest egg that they invest in risky schemes that can wind up saddling them with steep losses. Below we profile three retired individuals and one couple who have made some kind of major mistake in retirement planning and offer advice to help them recover from their gaffes. We also suggest strategies you should take to avoid making similar missteps en route to your own retirement.

Saving too little or late during your career. In 1988, at the age of 64, Arthur Anders of Sand Springs, Okla. was looking at a lean retirement. For 25 years, he had worked for two amusement companies, installing and maintaining jukeboxes and vending machines. Neither company had offered a pension. Then, in 1988, Anders' third employer, automotive supplies conglomerate Stewart Warner, shut down the Oklahoma operation where he had worked for the preceding 14 years. When he left, all he got was $30,000 of his own money that he had accumulated by contributing 3% of his salary to the employee retirement savings plan. A widower whose wife died of cancer in 1984, Anders says he was panicked about having to survive on little more than about $11,000 a year in Social Security payments. "I didn't have enough money, and I knew I had to do something," he explains.

His first tack was to find another job. Almost immediately, Anders landed a spot in sales paying $12,740 a year at the Pump Shop, a Tulsa automotive supply warehouse where he worked until last year. Alas, he received no pension benefits from this firm either. The next step was to grow his modest nest egg. In 1990, Anders invested 40% of his $30,000 in dividend-paying stocks such as Johnson & Johnson and Allegheny Power to generate income. For capital appreciation, he put another 20% of his money into blue-chip technology stocks like Microsoft and Intel. He plowed about 25% of his money into two stock index funds that invest in shares of large U.S. companies. He kept the remaining 15% in precious-metals stocks and a bank account.

Riding the bull market for the past seven years, Anders parlayed his savings into $210,000. That's a fabulous 32% return, more than double the 15% gain for stocks overall during the period. Believing the market was beginning to look shaky, Anders retreated to a more defensive position at the end of March, moving about $30,000 from growth stocks into shares of more stable utilities and energy companies like Enron. His nest egg now throws off about $1,500 a month in income that supplements the $900 he gets from Social Security. He owns his $120,000 house free and clear but still says that his income "is just barely enough to live on."

While Anders deserves praise for the impressive returns he's earned, he may be too dependent on today's high-flying U.S. stock market. By putting 15% to 20% of his portfolio into no-load international stock funds, Anders can improve his portfolio's long-term return as well as lower risk. To squeeze out a bit more income, Anders should consider putting 5% of his money into a so-called flexible bond fund that invests in corporate and government bonds as well as dividend-paying stocks.

How can you avoid Anders' blunder? Start by socking away as much as you can afford in employer-sponsored savings plans, such as 401(k)s. They let you invest pretax dollars that compound tax-free until you withdraw them at retirement. Most large and midsize companies offer such plans and also kick in half of what you contribute, for a typical maximum match of 3% of your salary. If your employer doesn't offer such a plan, or you have extra cash you can set aside, invest the maximum allowable $2,000 into an IRA. The gains you earn remain untaxed until you withdraw them even if you can't deduct your contribution from your taxable income. (The deduction begins phasing out at $40,000 of taxable income for married couples and $25,000 for singles.) If you've funded your IRA and you have even more money you can afford to put away for at least 15 years, consider tax-deferred variable annuities such as those offered by T. Rowe Price, USAA Life and Vanguard. As explained in detail in Chapter 4, annuities essentially are mutual funds with a tax shelter wrapping.

Investing blindly in can't miss schemes. Through careful saving, Gerald Kirschenberg and his wife Lillian were able to retire to Sunrise, Fla. in 1978 with a substantial retirement portfolio. "We were dancing in our swimming pool, saying 'We made it,'" recalls Lillian, a former Queens, N.Y. bookkeeper. Leery of speculating in the stock market, she and Gerald, a former owner of a men's clothing store, had safeguarded their funds in federally insured bank certificates of deposit. They then paid about 8%, which provided enough income for the couple to retire comfortably. By 1989, however, those CD rates had plunged to just 4%.

The Kirschenbergs panicked. What if they didn't have enough money to last the rest of their lives? Then an Advest stockbroker they had never met came cold-calling and offered a supposedly safe investment with a tax-advantaged return starting at 10.5% and rising to 12% in the sixth year. The couple went for it. At the broker's urging, the Kirschenbergs contend, they cashed in some of their low-paying CDs and in 1989 invested $28,500 in two equipment-leasing limited partnerships.

They have received a 12% payout from one of the partnerships for the past seven years. But they say the payments on the other, called PLM Equipment Growth Fund IV, declined from 10.5% in 1991 to as low as 2.5% in 1994. Worse, the couple didn't realize that part of the income they got from both partnerships was actually a return of their own principal, which is why they didn't owe tax on it. That alleged deception, plus Advest's supposed assertions that the partnerships were safe, are two reasons why the Kirschenbergs and dozens of other elderly investors have filed an arbitration complaint for fraud against

Advest for the PLM partnerships. The investors' lawyer also charges that the PLM partnerships took fees and expenses of almost 20% off the top before investing any money. In response, Advest counsel William Freitag says the firm's brokers provided prospectuses that outlined the terms of the partnerships. But now that investors are disappointed with the results of the investment, he says, they want to hold Advest responsible. "We are fighting the complaint," adds Freitag.

The Kirschenbergs are resigned to the likelihood that it could take years before their case is resolved. In the meantime, their attorney estimates that the partnerships are worth only about 20% of their original price. "Fortunately, we haven't had to modify our standard of living, though we did want to leave that money to our kids," says Lillian. Their experience has convinced them never to move out of bank CDs again, particularly now that rates for five-year CDs have risen into the 6% to 7% range. But their strategy is shortsighted because both Lillian and Gerald could live another 20 years. The income they get from CDs won't keep up with inflation. As an inflation hedge, the couple should gradually move 15% to 30% of their savings into conservative stock funds that invest in a blend of large-company stocks and high-grade bonds. These funds probably won't get hammered in market squalls. And they can deliver solid growth of capital over the long term.

How can you avoid this mistake? Maintain a portfolio that divides your money among stocks, bonds and cash so you won't have to resort to esoteric investments promising plump payoffs quickly. The precise mix will vary depending on your age and stomach for risk. But even elderly investors ought to keep some of their money in stocks. True, stocks are likely to deliver a bumpier ride along with higher returns. If you are at least 20 years from retirement, you should consider putting 75% or more of your assets in stocks because you will have many years to recover from market swoons. If you're recently retired, keep close to 50% in stocks. You will need inflation-whipping growth to make your money last as long as you do. And just say no to any pitch for an investment that is supposed to be safe and generate a double-digit return. That goes double when you hear one peddled over the phone by someone you don't know.

Leaving money matters to your spouse. Pat Patton, 79, never gave much thought to herself, much less her retirement. She left the finances to her husband Jack. Pat started working in 1960 as a volunteer at a nonprofit children's nature museum in Charlotte, N.C. Then she took a full-time job there in 1965. In 1979, Jack quit his job as a chemist with Pennwalt Chemicals because of worsening emphysema. The next year, Pat took a job at Discovery Place, a science museum in Charlotte, and eventually became an administrative assistant earning $18,000 a year. For a while, the couple were able to manage on her salary, plus the $920 they received monthly from Jack's Social Security payments and his $500-a-month company pension. By 1987, however, Jack's breathing became so bad that he didn't have the strength to drive and fell into a depression. Selflessly, Pat quit her job to spend time with him. "I wanted to make his last years happy ones," she says.

After Jack died in 1990, Pat stopped getting his pension because her husband had not signed up for the joint-and-survivor option that would have paid lifetime benefits for both spouses. So at the age of 71, Pat realized she would receive only $984 a month from her own Social Security earnings. She wasn't sure she could live on that. "Most women should pay much more attention to their finances than I did," she says. So Pat jumped at a friend's offer of a temporary spot in the office at Garden Secrets, a local plant store. The assignment soon turned permanent, and now Patton can count on a salary of about $22,000 a year. The job turned out to be a blessing in another way–it keeps her occupied. "So many of my friends are unhappy in retirement. They have nothing to do all day," she says.

Patton, however, needs another source of money in case illness or advancing age prevents her from working. The $75,000 equity in her condominium is her only significant asset. Thus the solution may be to take out a so-called reverse mortgage that's described in "Tap the Old Homestead for Income" in Chapter 3. She could draw against her home equity with a $30,000 to $40,000 credit line or receive monthly payments of $300 to $450 from a lender. When she dies and the house is sold, the lender will get first dibs on the proceeds.

How can you sidestep this pitfall? You and your spouse should meet with your financial planner or accountant to complete a need analysis. It forecasts your likely future expenses year by year and shows whether they will exceed your projected income from sources such as work, your pensions and investments. If the expected outflow exceeds resources, boost your savings to bridge the gap. If it appears you may still have a shortfall, consider adding to your life insurance. And it's generally smart to have your spouse choose the joint-and-survivor option for pension benefits. This guarantees that the checks will keep coming after his or her death. Note that women live about seven years longer than men, on average. So this move can be especially crucial for them.

Choosing the wrong place to live. Four years ago, Juanita Rippetoe, now 69, and her husband Bill, then an owner of a car-leasing business, retired to a dream house they had built in the suburbs of Fort Worth. Four months after they moved in, Bill died of a heart attack. After that, Nita says, "I hated the house. It brought me nothing but sadness." Her relatives urged Nita to move to Houston to be near them and directed the search for a new place, picking out a $147,000 three-bedroom house in a new gated community in Katy, which is about 10 miles outside of Houston. "It's an elegant house," Rippetoe says, "but it was a big mistake." Only a few other houses have sold, so Rippetoe doesn't have many neighbors. She doesn't see her relatives much either because they work full time. She feels marooned. "Every time I go to an aerobics class or play bridge, I have to drive a long way," Nita says. She would like to move to Houston or even back to Fort Worth, where she has friends. But with new homes moving at a glacial pace in her subdivision, she would probably have to take a 15% loss to unload her house.

Rippetoe has not let the housing error sink her retirement. She fights off isolation by involving herself in a whirl of activities–bridge, exercise, volunteer and church work. Still lonely, particularly in the evenings, Nita feels that a gentleman friend might be the best solution to her problem. "A lot of men my age seem to want a nurse or a purse," she says with a laugh. "But I'm looking." But retreating to Fort Worth may not ease Rippetoe's melancholy. She has been away for most of the past four years. So she may no longer have that much in common with her friends there. Instead, Rippetoe might consider selling her home when the housing market revives, investing the proceeds and then moving to an apartment in a thriving neighborhood such as a section of downtown Houston that's known as The Galleria.

How can you avoid this mistake? Before relocating to a retirement paradise, rent an apartment or house in the area to see whether you like living there. Widows should be cautious about uprooting soon after a husband's death. In their grief, they often rely on a child or another relative to make decisions like selling the house or moving to a new city. Then they wind up in places that don't particularly suit them.

2

WHERE TO

INVEST IN

TODAY'S

MARKETS

William Martin, Federal Reserve Board chairman from 1951 to 1970, aptly described his job as being "the chaperone who takes away the punch bowl when the party gets going good." In other words, the central bank raises short-term interest rates to dry up the flow of money, which sobers up the economy and stock market. Given the gala stock gains of recent years, investors would have to acknowledge that today's Fed chairman, Alan Greenspan, has been a generous host. In 1995 and 1996, he reduced short-term rates three times for a total of three-quarters of a percentage point. As a result, with corporate profits growing more than 10% a year, lower interest rates spurred the Dow Jones industrial average to gains of more than 80%.

In late March, however, Greenspan decided that the economy's continued strength might lead to higher inflation and hiked interest rates by a quarter of a point. Odds are he will boost them again. On 11 of the 13 occasions that the Fed has increased rates since 1936, it has raised them again a median of roughly four months later. "Greenspan's move signals the end of easy profits in the stock market," says strategist Rao Chalasani at Everen Securities in Chicago. Share prices don't always dive the first time the Fed raises rates after a period of easy money. Based on historic patterns, however, here's what to expect.

Prepare for subpar returns from stocks. When shares are priced at earnings multiples above 17, as they were recently, they typically return less than 7% annually during the next five years. That pace is four percentage points below their average annual return since 1926. In contrast, top-quality bonds and other income investments could well outperform stocks over the next couple of years. Although interest rate hikes may temporarily depress bond prices 5% or so, they probably will rebound later this year. Here's why. Greenspan's policies will likely slow the economy, allowing long-term rates to ease to around 6%, down from their recent 7% levels. That will boost bond prices as much as 10% above current levels.

As a result, most investors should rebalance their retirement portfolio holdings of stocks and income investments. Don't give up on stocks, of course. During the next 10 to 20 years, they will remain your best choice for building wealth and saving for retirement. But the enormous gains of the past two years may have left your portfolio too heavily invested in stocks. By moving money out of your most overpriced and vulnerable stocks and into bonds and other income investments, you can slash your risk as much as 33%. Even better, such a balanced portfolio figures to earn at least as much as stocks over the next five years.

Why stocks are 15% to 20% overpriced. Despite the stock market's huge gains in 1995 (up 38%) and 1996 (up 23%) and the first half of 1997 (up about 22%), it won't be able to deliver anywhere near such fat returns during the next five years or so. "The market posts three double-digit years in a row only three times in a century," notes Hugh Johnson, chief investment officer at First Albany in Albany, N.Y. Moreover, most bellwethers are now signaling trouble ahead for stocks, which are expensive by almost every measure. The average PE (price-earnings) multiple of Standard & Poor's 400 industrial companies stands around 20, fully 40% above the norm. And those stocks yield a stingy 1.8%, less than half the 70-year average. "Given these valuations, the market has almost no upside potential, compared with a downside of 40%," says Jim Floyd, senior analyst at Leuthold/Weeden Research, an investment advisory firm in Minneapolis.

Corporate earnings growth also seems to be slowing. Most economists expect that profits, which grew an average of almost 10% annually from 1990 through 1996, will rise only about two-thirds as much this year. Merrill Lynch economist Bruce Steinberg forecasts that earnings will increase a mere 7% in 1997 and only 4% in 1998. Meanwhile, inflation and interest rates could start creeping up. Since 1990, inflation has fallen from an annualized 6% to around 3%; short-term interest rates have come down from nearly 8% to 5.4%. "Because rising labor costs and high consumer demand could push inflation above its current 3% level, Greenspan may have to raise interest rates another 0.25 to 0.5 percentage point," says Salomon Bros. economist Brian Jones. As a result, the stock market is long overdue for a correction. Stock prices have risen for more than six years without dipping more than 10%. Since 1945, the average time between 10% pullbacks in the market has been only 19 months.

Why the market isn't headed for a crash. Some strategists warn that a market collapse of as much as 30% is imminent. But you probably don't need to worry that share prices will take a sudden dive as they did in the crash of 1987. Although stocks are at least as overpriced as they were before that plunge, high prices alone don't cause a crash. Long-term interest rates also have to rise high enough to draw investors' money out of stocks. In 1987, 30-year Treasury yields soared from 7.6% to 10.2% in the eight months before the crash. By contrast, rates have remained in a fairly stable range, generally between 6.5% and 7%, over the past year. While Greenspan's short-term rate hike could push bond yields up half a point or so in the next six months, "bond yields could drop to 6% sometime in mid-1998," says William Gross, managing director of Pacific Investment Management in Newport Beach, Calif. (See his views on bonds later in this chapter.) In that kind of rate environment, share prices could temporarily pull back 15% or more. But a devastating drop is unlikely.

How to buttress your portfolio. "In the long run, the key to making more money is to lose less in periods of decline," says William Dawson, chief of fixed-income investments at Federated Investors in Pittsburgh. With many growth stocks looking increasingly vulnerable, you might consider lower-risk companies or stock funds such as those discussed later in this chapter. In addition, you might cut your risk by diversifying into other investments. To see the benefits of defensive diversification, consider the results of the MONEY Small Investor Index, a model portfolio that reflects the average adult's investment holdings. Over the past 25 years, this fairly conservative portfolio has returned nearly 10% a year with only about half the stock market's risk. Active investors typically keep more than 60% of their money in the market. But today's Small Investor Index portfolio has only 50% of total assets in stocks. Most of the rest is invested in income investments, with 20% in bonds and 30% in money-market funds and other cash investments.

Such a cash-heavy portfolio is particularly appropriate for people close to retirement or in need of regular income. Still, no matter what your stage of life, it makes sense to unload the most volatile stocks with PEs above 17, the recent average for the S&P 500 index. Put the proceeds in income investments, such as bonds, utility stocks and REITs (real estate investment trusts). Adjusting your portfolio has become critically important simply because the market's gains have thrown most investors' holdings out of balance. The fact that stocks have soared in the past two years means that a portfolio originally composed of 65% stocks, 25% bonds and 10% cash is now probably 73% stocks, 20% bonds and 7% cash.

At the very least, a sensible investor would sell 10% of his or her stocks and shift the money into bonds and cash. If you want to make your portfolio more than usually defensive, you could reasonably move 20% or 25% of your stockholdings into income investments. As a general rule, the shorter an income investment's maturity, the less risky it is. That applies to Treasuries, zeros and municipal bonds alike. For example, if interest rates rise one percentage point, 20-year Treasuries would lose 6%. Five- to 10-year issues would lose only about 2%.

Foreign stocks are also a worthwhile alternative if you're paring down your domestic stock portfolio, says Douglas Johnson, senior international investment strategist at Merrill Lynch. First, there are near-ly always foreign markets that deliver better returns than the U.S. Last year, U.S. stock prices rose 23%. Yet the U.S. market lagged behind several others, including Brazil (53%), Finland (37%), Sweden (34%) and Hong Kong (33%). Second, foreign stocks offer global diversification. When the U.S. market zigs, another that's either large or small, or east or west, may zag. So spreading your investments across several world markets dampens your portfolio's volatility.

◆ MONITOR THESE FINANCIAL TRENDS

Our outlook assumes a fair degree of economic stability here and abroad. But any number of unforeseen events could alter our view. The greatest danger in the U.S. would be an upsurge in inflation to well above 3.2%. The other domestic threat to the economy is the possibility, albeit remote, that Federal Reserve chairman Alan Greenspan might trigger a recession by mistakenly pushing interest rates too high.

There are also two possible negative developments overseas that would be serious enough to really undermine U.S. stocks. The first would be a spike in oil prices to well above the recent $21 a barrel in response to political instability or war in the Middle East. The second negative turn would be recession in Western Europe. Such a slowdown could come as several European countries attempt to cut government spending to meet the deficit targets required for membership in the proposed European Monetary Union. No forecast, of course, can factor in such speculative possibilities. Odds are they won't happen. So here's a detailed explanation of what we do see ahead.

The cost of labor will keep rising.
Today's chief threat to the U.S. economy is higher labor costs. Average hourly earnings are in line with the 3% annual growth posted by wages and salaries since 1993. But couple that increase with low unemployment, as well as with labor shortages in some regions, and you've got a recipe for rising costs. Unions under the aggressive new leadership of AFL-CIO chief John Sweeney also seem certain to fight harder for a bigger slice of corporate profits.

Productivity appears to have peaked.
Rising salaries, wages and benefits don't automatically boost a company's labor costs if workers also become more productive. That's a big if these days. Productivity was inching up at only a 0.4% annual rate lately. By contrast, productivity growth has averaged about 1% a year since 1989. "Such gains are weakest in services, and more than 80% of jobs today are in services," says economist Robert Brusca at Nikko Securities in New York City. Moreover, as the U.S. job market continues to shift away from manufacturing to services, where efficiencies are harder to come by, the drag on productivity will worsen.

Inflation isn't dead after all.
Companies might be tempted to try to pass on their higher labor costs to consumers by raising prices. But given the intense competition that U.S. corporations face in today's global economy, businesses that boost prices will risk losing sales. "Competitive market conditions prevent companies from raising prices that much," says Merrill Lynch economist Bruce Steinberg. Even so, some price hikes will stick, pushing up inflation from 3% a year to 3.2%. Inflation will remain tame only if the federal budget deficit does-

n't start to rise again. Since 1992, President Clinton has slashed the deficit significantly. Keeping the deficit on a diet, however, is getting harder because entitlements such as Medicare keep costing more. We expect that Clinton and the Republican Congress will cooperate on deficit reduction. But that has a catch too. Spending cuts might crimp economic growth.

The economy will start to sputter. Whatever policies the government pursues during the next year or two, the economy seems headed for a slowdown. A key reason is the Federal Reserve's tight-money stance over the past three years. The top chart on the next page shows how short-term interest rates compare with the levels economists would expect in light of the inflation rate. As you can see, Federal Reserve chairman Greenspan hiked interest rates sharply several years ago and has kept them comparatively high ever since. We thought these elevated rates would slow the economy in 1997. Instead, growth in GDP (gross domestic product) surged to a stunning 5.8% annualized rate in the first quarter. But we still believe the economic slowdown has simply been postponed.

Plump profit margins will be squeezed. Shortly after the recovery from the 1990-91 recession began, corporate profit margins started to soar (see the top chart on page 29). Sales were expanding 5% a year. But labor costs were growing at a mere 2.8%. As a result, earnings for the corporations that make up the S&P 500 index more than doubled to $75 billion over the past five years. In 1997, however, margins are likely to be pushed down by exactly the opposite trends. Revenue growth for U.S. businesses will slow along with the economy. And companies will have to absorb labor cost increases without raising prices much. "After labor costs start rising, profit margins will narrow," says Steinberg. Such a margin squeeze won't cause an outright decline in corporate profits but will rein in their growth.

Interest rates could head lower. An economic slowdown will bring some good news in the form of lower interest rates. Fed chairman Greenspan might hike rates again in 1997 if he sees signs that the economy is too strong. But such a rate increase would amount to half a percentage point at the most. Moreover, once an economic slowdown is clearly under way, we expect that Greenspan will ease short-

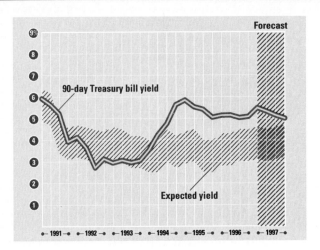

...BUT INTEREST RATES WILL FADE

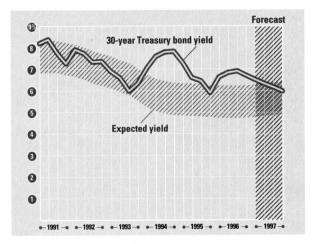

Sources: Bloomberg Information Services, MONEY estimates

Interest rates have been too high since 1994, when Federal Reserve chairman Alan Greenspan hiked short-term rates to slow the economy and pre-empt a rise in inflation. As the top chart shows, since late 1994 short-term rates have remained about a percentage point above the range economists figure is customary given the rate of inflation. Greenspan's tight money has also kept bond yields higher than expected levels (see the bottom chart). Once the economy slows, the Fed will be able to let short-term rates ease. Long rates could decline to 6.25%.

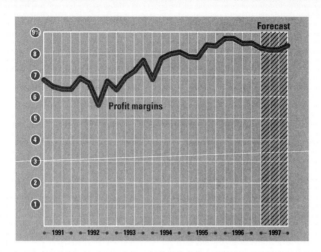

...AND UNDERMINE '97 EARNINGS

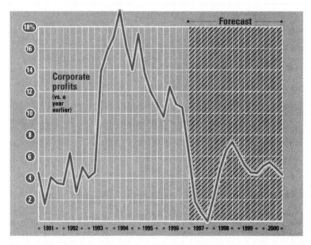

Sources: Bloomberg Information Services, DRI/McGraw-Hill, Merrill Lynch, MONEY estimates

Companies will not offset rising labor costs by raising prices because consumers will resist paying more. As a result, higher labor expenses will have to come out of corporate earnings. Profit margins, which have been rising since 1992, could fall half a point in 1997 (see the top chart). A small drop in margins won't cause an earnings decline. But the squeeze will rein in profit growth (see the bottom chart). The likely result? As companies report earnings that are lower than what shareholders are hoping for, share prices could temporarily fall 15% to 20%.

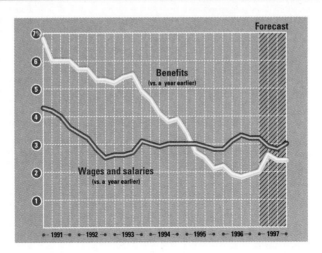

...WILL PUSH UP INFLATION A TAD

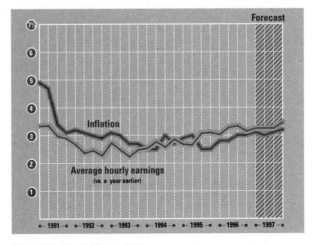

Sources: Merrill Lynch, MONEY estimates

The most important cause of inflation—a rise in labor costs—is starting to worry investors. Since 1993, wages and salaries have risen 3% or so annually. But as the top chart shows, recently those increases have been offset by smaller ones in the cost of benefits. This year, however, average hourly earnings, including wages, salaries and benefits, are expected to grow faster than inflation, which has risen 3% over the past 12 months (see the bottom chart). In response, inflation will likely be pushed up to roughly a 3.2% annual rate by the end of 1997.

term rates, bringing yields on 90-day Treasury bills to below 5%. Most other interest rates on longer maturities would also begin to fade.

Bond prices are poised to rebound. Even a half point decline in interest rates would spark a bond market rally. Long-term Treasury bonds, zero-coupon issues and other income investments could offer investors relatively attractive total returns of 10% or more. "Stocks are so overpriced right now that a 10% total return on bonds looks like a better deal," says Steven Leuthold of Leuthold/Weeden Research in Minneapolis.

◆ BEWARE OF THE DOW'S HYPED PROFITS

Don't believe everything you read, particularly in corporate earnings reports. Our analysis of the Dow Jones industrial average suggests that accounting tricks are overstating the earnings of this 30-stock group by about 20%. Thus the Dow appears to be roughly 20% higher than it would be without such aggressive bookkeeping. These hyped profits have been inflating the Dow since 1991, when corporate chiefs became obsessed with a high-stakes game called earnings gap. That's the chasm between companies' true profits and the reported earnings on which most investors focus. This gamesmanship has led investors to overestimate the Dow companies' growth prospects and overpay for their shares. Expectations of ever-higher profits will become increasingly difficult for the 30 stocks to meet if the economy slows sometime in 1997. The result? The Dow could drop 15% to 20% within the next year.

Why one-time charges rarely are. This earnings gap can mainly be traced to something fittingly called GAAP (generally accepted accounting principles). GAAP is set largely by the Financial Accounting Standards Board (FASB), the chief rule-making body for the profession. These rules permit, and in some cases require, companies to take special charges against profits for such items as the cost of a failed venture or severance packages for laid-off workers. What's wrong with that? These special, nonrecurring losses are generally ignored by both analysts and shareholders. The charges are viewed as isolated one-time events even when companies seem to claim them every two or three years. As a rule, Wall Street analysts tend to smile on top executives who face up to their companies' biggest problems, quickly take steps to get beyond them and promise not to be boneheads again. Meanwhile, the company's accountants write off every cent the CEOs squandered.

The effects of this game can be quite pernicious. First, nonrecurring write-offs typically inflate earnings for the following year or two. That's because companies often use such charges as an opportunity to write off expenses today that ought to be subtracted from tomorrow's profits. Second, hyped earnings make the company appear to be growing faster than it really is. Third, all too often the company messes up again and takes another big write-off. Barton Biggs, chairman of New York City's Morgan Stanley Asset Management, frames the problem this way: "In some cases, companies take restructuring charges for legitimate reasons. But when you see more than two charges within five years, you should wonder whether the company is writing off ongoing expenses to inflate current or future profits."

The hidden costs of distorted earnings. This issue

wouldn't matter all that much if the amounts involved were relatively small. But beginning with the major corporate restructurings of the early 1990s, companies have abandoned all restraint. Jack Ciesielski, a Baltimore investment adviser, notes that 26 of the 30 Dow companies took restructuring charges between 1991 and 1995. Moreover, 21 Dow stocks took more than one charge during those years. Nine racked up total nonrecurring losses of more than $1 billion over the period, according to Ciesielski. The nine firms include IBM, which charged off $19.2 billion; AT&T, $8.6 billion; GM, $3.1 billion; Du Pont, $1.9 billion; Chevron, $1.8 billion; Kodak, $1.7 billion; Procter & Gamble, $1.7 billion; Sears, $1.7 billion; and United Technologies, $1.3 billion.

Noted accounting authority Abraham Briloff of New York City's Bernard Baruch College points out that the charges against earnings are 10 to 40 times larger than they were 20 years ago. He says: "Twenty years ago $50 million would have been a big number. Now people shrug off $2 billion." A billion here and a billion there, and pretty soon you're reporting misleading earnings. In response, officials at the Dow companies say it is unfair to compare the size of charges today to those of 20 years ago because their businesses have grown enormously since then. They also dispute that restructuring charges have distorted their earnings. In addition, they note that they report profits both with and without special charges. Finally, some say big charges were necessary to make their companies competitive.

Perhaps. But the effect of those charges on the Dow companies' balance sheets is staggering. They slashed the firms' combined equity (also known as book value) some 20%, compared with what it would have been had the restructuring charges not been taken. That's why we think the Dow is as much as 20% overvalued. It's as though a newsstand claimed to have had weekend sales of $1,000 but had only $800 in the till on Sunday night.

How much did IBM really earn? To see how repeated charges distort earnings, take a close look at IBM. From 1991 to 1993, IBM reported massive nonrecurring charges of $19.2 billion resulting from a complete restructuring program. By taking the write-offs, the company all but guaranteed that future earnings would look terrific. Sure enough, IBM's reported earnings were up more than 40% in each of the two years after the charges. Investors have obviously been impressed and bid up the stock. But shareholders should be more skeptical. The company's restructuring charges between 1991 and 1995 have totaled $6.3 billion more than its entire earnings during that same period. So how much is the company really making?

Many accounting experts say big nonrecurring charges will likely continue despite growing awareness of the distortions that they cause. FASB and its Emerging Issues Task Force have recently tightened rules for companies that write off restructuring costs. The new rules restrict what can be included in a charge and prohibit last-minute write-offs to obscure poor quarterly results. But critics say companies will simply take charges more frequently. FASB chairman Dennis Beresford disagrees. He says FASB's new guidelines have "improved the situation." He adds: "The increasing number of charges is an economic development, tied to the changing nature of industries." But the fact remains that more frequent charges would almost surely create more distorted earnings.

With or without accounting reforms, the earnings gap seems destined to grow for as long as analysts and investors continue to ignore nonrecurring losses. Oppenheimer & Co. strategist Michael Metz is one of the few Wall Street pros who argues that companies shouldn't be rewarded for taking write-offs. "When companies take a nonrecurring charge, the top managers are saying, 'We misused our capital,'" says Metz. Moreover, since many of the pros ignore the froth in corporate profits, most small investors do too. In fact, you have to be a careful reader of research reports even to be aware of many write-offs.

Even the highly regarded *Value Line Investment Survey* omits nonrecurring charges from its main earnings listings when its analysts believe the charges are truly one-time losses. The charges are instead relegated to mouse type in the footnotes. "It really poses a problem for us," says Value Line's Morton Siegel, who goes on to stress that investors should pay close attention to the footnotes. We would add that investors who ignore the earnings gap in today's overpriced stock market could be setting themselves up for a major mistake over the next year or two.

◆ LOW-RISK STOCKS FOR YOUR NEST EGG

Everyone who's investing for retirement faces a variation on this dilemma. How do you balance the need to grow your capital with a sensible aversion to losing it? One of the best solutions is to own stocks that offer both growth of earnings and growth of dividends. "Growth stocks that pay dividends are a winning combination for retirees," says Stanley Nabi of Wood, Struthers & Winthrop, a New York City money manager. Since stock prices ultimately follow the trajectory of earnings, a stock whose profits are growing faster than inflation tends to protect your purchasing power. If the company also faithfully boosts its dividend, it is generally a sign that the firm backs its profit statement with a robust balance sheet and plenty of cash. To identify such exemplars, we asked leading money managers and Wall Street analysts to recommend steadily growing companies with dividend yields exceeding the S&P 500's recent 1.7%. We eliminated any firm that failed to increase its dividend payouts annually over the past five years. Our top five selections are described below.

◆ **McCormick & Co.** (recently traded over the counter around $25; 2.4% yield). From 1993 through 1995, this $1.7 billion (annual sales) processor of spices and seasonings took a pounding as Australian rival Burns-Philp challenged its hegemony on supermarket shelves. Fighting back, McCormick repackaged its line of spice combinations aimed at novice chefs, fired up its advertising campaign and saw sales jump 40%. The firm also announced a two-year restructuring that will focus on the core businesses of supermarket sales and fast-food restaurants. As part of that strategic shift, the firm sold its Gilroy Foods subsidiary in 1996 for $263 million and used the proceeds to pay down some of its $630 million in debt.

County Natwest Securities food industry analyst David Nelson estimates the new prepackaged seasonings line alone could add about 5% to earnings this year and 7% in 1998. Meanwhile, fast-growing overseas markets are expected to add 5% to earnings over each of the next five years. The firm has increased dividends an average of 19% annually over the past nine years even during its troubles in the mid-1990s. While currency fluctuations could dampen overseas sales, Nelson thinks the firm's leaner profile, new product lines and recently announced plan to repurchase 10 million shares should lift the stock 25% over the next 12 months. That's a projected total return of almost 28%.

◆ **Federal National Mortgage Association** (New York Stock Exchange; around $44; 1.9% yield). This $357 billion (assets) government chartered corporation known as Fannie Mae is the nation's largest middleman for residential mortgages. The Washington, D.C. firm earns fees from lenders for buying their loans and repackaging them into mortgage-backed securities that account for a third of its $2.7 billion profits. It also collects interest on its own mortgage portfolio, source of about 66% of profits. Investors have recently worried that Congressional budget cutters might try to eliminate the firm's quasi-governmental status, which lets it borrow at interest rates much lower than private banks. But analysts say forget it. "Fannie Mae can argue that the low rates it offers help keep housing prices low," says analyst Charles Vincent at PNC Asset Management in Philadelphia. "The government isn't likely to tamper with that." Adds Smith Barney analyst Thomas O'Donnell: "This is a solid company that has been able to increase its dividend payout in each of the past nine years." He expects Fannie Mae's profits and dividends to grow at a 13% annual clip as more and more first-time home buyers and retirement downsizers take out mortgages. He also sees the shares rising 23% in a year and earning a 25% total return.

◆ **Banc One** (NYSE; around $49; 3.1% yield). This Columbus, Ohio bank holding company, the nation's tenth largest with $102 billion in assets, grows by gobbling up smaller competitors. Banc One has made 113 acquisitions over the past 29 years, bringing the firm's total to 65 banks with over 1,500 offices in 12 states. Company president Richard Lehmann uses those mergers to streamline operations. The big payoff is an expected $328 million savings in operating costs in 1998. In the meantime, Banc One has added heft to its credit card division, which supplied 14% of profits in 1996, by acquiring First USA, the fourth largest issuer of Visas and Mastercards in the U.S. Are today's record levels of credit card delinquencies a concern? Not really, says Nabi, adding: "Even if interest rates continue to rise, the variable rates Banc One charges credit card and other customers will rise as well." Joseph Morford, a bank analyst at Alex. Brown in San Francisco, notes that the firm has increased dividends every year since 1987. He also predicts that profits will compound a brisk 14% annually over the next five years, elevating the stock 20% in a year and earning a 24% total return.

◆   **May Department Stores** (NYSE; around $48; 2.5% yield). This $12 billion company is prospering in a tough retail environment by deftly operating department stores such as Lord & Taylor, Filene's, Hecht's and Robinsons-May. The key is a marketing strategy that targets cost-conscious baby boomers, explains Roger DeBard, manager of Hotchkis & Wiley Balanced Income fund. "They've become bargain hunters now that they have to keep up with mortgage payments and save for college and retirement," he says. The company is actively pumping up its square footage to accommodate those customers, spending $200 million last year to expand and renovate 34 existing outlets. Retail analyst Joseph Ronning of Brown Brothers Harriman in New York City thinks the expansions can increase sales 13% annually over the next five years, while new outlets could add 8% to 9% to the top line. The fact that the company has increased dividends and per-share earnings in each of the past 22 years should reassure conservative investors. Ronning sees May's stock appreciating 15% in a year and producing a total return of nearly 18%.

◆   **Lincoln National** (NYSE; around $66; 3% yield). This $7.2 billion (assets) firm sells life insurance, annuities and property/casualty insurance as well as managing $50 billion in pension accounts. Angling to capture some of the billions of dollars baby boomers will continue to set aside for retirement, Lincoln has begun expanding its highly profitable money management division and unloading its more volatile property/casualty unit. In February, the firm agreed to buy $2.8 billion Voyageur Fund Managers, a tax-free bond fund company. In May, the company sold off 17% of its American States property/casualty unit for an estimated $600 million. Hotchkis & Wiley's DeBard expects the rest of the unit to follow sometime this year. Lincoln has boosted dividends in each of the past 13 years. Moreover, the stock's recent 3.7% yield is twice that of the market's. Edward Spehar at Lehman Brothers in New York City expects earnings to rise 13% in 1997 and 15% annually over the following two years. He sees the stock rising 13% in a year and earning a 17% total return.

◆ PRUDENT WAYS TO BET ON ASIA'S BOOM

Today's ever-industrious inhabitants of Asia's Pacific Rim are making economic strides in one generation that took people in the West more than a century to achieve. Already the standard of living is higher in Singapore and Hong Kong, where annual per capita gross domestic product tops $23,000, than in the United Kingdom ($18,913). This prosperity comes at a price, of course. The gap between rich and poor is immense. In Hong Kong, where there are more Rolls-Royces per capita than any place on earth, the poorest residents sleep and keep their few possessions in small cubicles with gratings. Real estate prices have risen out of the reach of most working people. Consider almost any upscale neighborhood in Hong Kong, a city seemingly unfazed by its return to Chinese rule on July 1. You will find tight little one-bedroom flats that rent for the equivalent of $2,000 to $10,000 a month.

None of these problems, however, changes the fact that Asia is a place of soaring hopes and boundless enterprise. The rapidly developing countries and economies of the Pacific Rim, including Hong Kong, Indonesia, Malaysia, the Philippines, Singapore, Taiwan and Thailand, are all expanding much faster than the U.S. Below we describe several ways that investors can try to ride the coattails of Asia's economic upturn. The two safest approaches, in fact, don't even require that you invest outside the good old U.S.A.

Buy U.S. blue chips with hefty Asian sales. With

American corporate profits projected to increase only 7% or so this year and next, many top U.S. growth stocks have to rely on foreign business to keep their profits expanding briskly. The best place to find earnings growth of 15% a year or better is in Asia. Here are two stocks that are heavily involved in that region.

American International Group (NYSE, around $147) has longstanding connections in Asia dating back to the company's 1919 founding in Shanghai. AIG now ranks as the the largest international commercial insurer in the U.S., with assets of $152 billion. And it derives at least half of its business overseas, including 38% from Asia. "The company's skill at building a financial services operation in emerging markets is unparalleled," says analyst Alice Schroeder at Oppenheimer & Co. in New York City. "The stock is expensive," adds analyst Robert Becker at Argus Research in New York City. "But it's a great long-term play." He thinks that developing economies such as China will be great markets for insurance. "First, you worry about creating wealth; then you worry about keeping it," he reasons. Schroeder rates the stock a buy and believes it can rise at least 15% over the next 12 months. "Earnings would hold up fairly well in a domestic downturn, and foreign operations are gaining visibility," says the analyst.

Boeing (NYSE, around $55) figures to get more than 30% of its estimated $35 billion sales this year from Asia. "China is the fastest-growing market in the industry," notes Merrill Lynch analyst Byron Callan. Adds analyst Jack Modzelewski at Paine Webber: "Over the next decade, the demand for aircraft will grow 3% to 4% annually in North America but 8% to 10% in the Pacific Rim." In addition to the company's bright prospects in Asia, Boeing is expanding its share of the domestic market. In March, for instance, Delta Air Lines announced it would make Boeing its sole aircraft supplier. "Boeing now has exclusives with airlines that own 10% of the world's fleet," says Callan, and it does business with virtually every carrier. He expects the stock to appreciate at least 25% over the next 12 months.

Bet on global producers of raw materials.

Commodity producers can cash in on the Asia boom without even leaving home. "Growth in Asia is the driving force behind the demand for copper, nickel and aluminum," says Smith Barney analyst Victor Lazarovici. And because the markets for oil and most other commodities are global, higher demand anywhere pushes up prices everywhere. As a result, commodity producers can profit from Pacific Rim growth even if they don't sell lots of goods in that region. To figure out which stocks to buy, just ask yourself the following question. If you were living in a shack with nothing more than a bed and stove, what would you want most? Probably electricity and a motor scooter. The first requires miles of copper wire and the second burns gasoline. Some of the top producers of each are U.S. companies.

Phelps Dodge (NYSE, around $83) is one of the world's strongest as well as biggest copper producers, with $3.7 billion in sales. The U.S. consumes about 20 pounds of copper per person a year. In China the figure is around two pounds per capita. "Asia's potential for copper consumption is mind boggling," says analyst Andrew O'Conor at brokerage Deutsche Morgan Grenfell in New York City. Both O'Conor and Lazarovici think the stock could gain at least 15% over the next 12 months. Also consider **Apache** (NYSE, around $33). Over the next three years, $1.1 billion Apache's oil and gas production will grow 11% annually, says analyst Thomas Lewis at Nesbitt Burns Securities in Chicago. The company is also active in the Far East energy market. "By the turn of the century, oilfields in Australia and Indonesia will probably account for 8% to 10% of Apache's total production volume," says analyst Paul Korus at Petrie Parkman in Denver. Both analysts figure the shares could rise about 25% over the next 12 months.

Buy regional funds at big discounts.

The most convenient way to invest directly in Asian stocks is through diversified funds that buy a cross section of top companies. Regular open-end funds are one way to go. But an even smarter choice is a closed-end fund selling at a double-digit discount. A closed-end has a fixed number of shares that trade on a stock exchange. The price that investors are willing to pay for fund shares, however, can vary considerably from the underlying value of the portfolio's holdings. Many Asian funds lately were selling at discounts exceeding 10%. We recommend two below.

Fidelity Advisor Emerging Asia (NYSE, around $14), which has none of its $140 million assets in Japan or Australia, is a pure play on the fastest-growing Asian countries. "The portfolio was up 19% last year because the fund was better than most of its rivals at avoiding poor-performing markets," says Smith Barney analyst Michael Porter. Over the next 12 months, he thinks the fund could return about 20%. Also take a look at **Morgan Stanley Asia Pacific** (NYSE, around $10). Morgan Stanley's blue-chip Asian fund has been trading near its low for the past year largely because it was nearly 40% invested in the long-depressed Japanese stock market. But that bet may be about to pay off. "The seven-year Japanese bear market is coming to an end," says strategist Rao Chalasani at Everen Securities in Chicago. "Interest rates are low now, and asset prices are no longer inflated." He thinks a portfolio like this one could return 20% or more over two years.

Own Asian blue chips that trade in the U.S. The potentially most profitable approach is to buy shares of individual Asian companies. As a rule, it's best to focus on the 350 or so Asian issues that trade in the U.S. as American Depositary Receipts, which are ownership rights to foreign stocks held by large banks. Here are two that analysts recommend.

Philippine Long Distance Telephone (NYSE, around $63), as well as other phone companies in Asia's emerging markets, are often viewed as proxies for these economies because they provide a service essential for businesses. Some analysts caution, however, that changes in the international price structure could hurt profits for Asian phone companies over the next three years. But stiff increases in domestic rates are offsetting the erosion in international long distance, says Merrill Lynch analyst Craig Irvine based in Singapore. He sees Philippine Long Distance gaining 17% within 12 months. One impetus, says international economist David Malpass at Bear Stearns in New York City, "is that the Philippines has recorded four straight years of accelerating growth." And, he adds, "We expect this market to perform strongly in 1997."

Bank of East Asia (traded over the counter, around $3.45) is poised to expand its lending 20% annually over the next four years, predicts analyst Elan Cohen at J.P. Morgan's Hong Kong office. One reason is that Hong Kong–based BEA is the most profitable foreign bank operating on the mainland and plans to go from six branches in China to 20 by the year 2000. Some analysts worry that the Hong Kong market may suffer a temporary decline of 10% or so this year. So they would wait and try to buy the stock closer to $3. Note, however, that the bank's ADR is not listed in most newspaper stock tables. To monitor the price, grab a Wall Street Journal, look up the stock on the Hong Kong exchange and divide that price by the U.S. dollar exchange rate (fixed at 7.7). That may be a bother. But it's a small price to broaden your investment horizons in Asia.

◆ FUNDS THAT WIN BIG BY NOT LOSING

With stock prices doubling and then doubling again in the past decade, you would think that dozens of stock funds had racked up 10 straight moneymaking years. Well think again. During that period, calculates Morningstar, about 190 diversified stock and balanced portfolios have been run by the same manager or at least one management team member. But only seven cruised through that high-flying stretch without posting a loss in any calendar year.

What made this feat so devilishly difficult were three separate tough years. In 1987, some 67 of those stock funds in our original group lost money in the wake of the Dow's single-day 22% meltdown that October. In the recession-plagued year of 1990, when the typical stock portfolio dropped 5.7%, another 154 of the stock funds slipped into the negative column. In 1994, Federal Reserve interest-rate hikes kept a lid on stock prices. Stock funds as a group fell 1.5%, and 101 ended the year in the red.

Below we profile the seven stock funds that defied the odds to post 10-year winning streaks. Those stalwarts employ a variety of strategies to stay in the black. Brandywine, the only one of our choices that is more volatile than the norm for stock funds, seeks out rapidly growing small and large companies. FPA Paramount manager Bill Sams keeps a hefty cash position and buys undervalued stocks. Franklin Growth I, Nationwide and Investment Company of America invest in large-company stocks. Dodge & Cox Balanced blends stocks and bonds. And Analytic Optioned Equity uses a sophisticated options trading strategy to keep an even keel during market squalls.

Reliable gainers like our seven wonders are compelling buys for retirement portfolios now that MONEY thinks stocks are poised to suffer a 15% to 20% correction. No stock fund, of course, is immune to market downdrafts. While these seven have avoided calendar-year losses in the past decade, they have had to ride out many short-term setbacks. Brandywine, for example, tumbled about 40% from September through November 1987, when the S&P 500 skidded 30%. Only two funds featured here (Brandywine and FPA Paramount) have managed the doubly daunting coup of avoiding annual losses and outpacing the S&P 500 during the past decade.

Brandywine. Talk about a spotless record. Manager Foster Friess and his crew of 25 colleagues have not had a calendar-year loss at this growth fund since they launched it in 1985. True, Brandywine (800-656-3017) barely squeaked by in 1994 with a minuscule return that translated into a $5 gain on a $25,000 investment–the fund's minimum initial ante. But why quibble? Brandywine's nearly 16% annualized return for the past 10 years handily outpaced the S&P 500's 13%. Friess and Co. have compiled their enviable record by ferreting out firms they believe can exploit a new product, service or management change to boost annual earnings by 20% or more. These days, the squad has 40% of the portfolio's assets invested in technology companies including computer maker Gateway 2000 and semiconductor giant Intel. Note that Brandywine has taken 34% more risk than the norm for stock funds over the past 10 years, according to Morningstar's proprietary risk measure that calculates how often and by how much a fund's monthly performance lags the return of 90-day Treasury bills. So this portfolio would seem the most likely of our seven picks to break its streak during an extended market correction. Still, as Friess points out, risk has its rewards: "I have long maintained that higher volatility brings better long-term returns."

FPA Paramount. Manager Bill Sams has proved that you don't need volatility to beat the market. Sams has guided FPA Paramount (800-982-4372) to an index-beating 14% annualized gain during the past 10 years while taking 32% less risk than the norm. Fund aficionados usually had to admire his work from afar because the fund was closed to new investors for all but three months of that stretch. Sams swung open the door to new investors in February and says he will keep it ajar at least until assets hit $1 billion or so (vs. about $750 million lately). Paramount's low-risk, high-reward formula combines a hefty cash stake with a concentrated portfolio of only two dozen stocks that Sams believes are priced below their intrinsic value. He recently turned his attention to the moribund gold sector, plunking 12% of fund assets into Homestake Mining, Newmont Mining and Placer Dome. "We're starting to see consolidations in the industry, which is a plus," says Sams. "Besides, I don't see much risk other than that these stocks might move sideways rather than go up."

Sams has not had a losing calendar year since he first arrived at Paramount in November 1981. His closest call was a 1.6% gain in 1990, a year when stock funds fell almost 6%. The fund has also held up better than its peers during market declines. Paramount's 22% drop during the tumultuous September through November 1987 stretch was far less painful than the 30% drop for the S&P 500. Not that Sams is invincible. Paramount's 13% 1995 return, for example, lagged the market by 25 points. Stick around for an extended period that includes both market climbs and collapses, though, and Sams is the man. For the past 15 years, FPA Paramount ranks as the No. 1 portfolio among the 73 growth and income funds Morningstar tracked over that stretch.

Wary of today's blimpish stock prices, Sams has stashed about 37% of his fund assets in cash. That's more than five times the average for stock funds. But even that hefty amount pales in comparison to 1973, when Sams moved 60% of the pension assets he was managing into cash just as the market was tanking. "I'm not calling for a collapse right now, but I do think we are playing with fire," says the 30-year investment vet. "If the market continues to go up, my shareholders will participate. And if it goes down, we should not be hurt as badly."

Franklin Growth. Manager Jerry Palmieri adds a new dimension to buy and hold. "In a perfect world, I would keep a stock forever," says Palmieri. "That would mean I was right on its long-term growth prospects." He's right a lot. Palmieri has typically held an investment for more than 20 years, vs. about a year for stock fund managers as a group. His portfolio still includes a handful of securities including Pfizer, Eastman Kodak and Minnesota Mining that Palmieri bought back in 1965 when he assumed control of the fund. Sticking with such reliable earners helped Franklin Growth (800-342-5236) return nearly 13% annually over the past 10 years, keeping it just behind the S&P 500 while incurring 25% less risk than the norm. Franklin Growth's last losing year was 1981, when its 5% slide matched the S&P 500's.

Palmieri protects his shareholders from losses by hunkering down in cash, which recently was 28% of assets, when he sees the market going head over heels. And his preference for established companies with sustainable earnings growth of 10% to 15% annually also helps to buttress the portfolio. This strategy may strike some investors as passionless. But Palmieri doesn't mind. "I've been called the Lawrence Welk of the investing business, and that's fine with me," he says. "My shareholders know we won't fall apart on the downside."

Nationwide. Manager Chuck Bath has posted profits in 12 consecutive years since taking charge of the fund in 1985. His portfolio of large growth companies that dominate their markets, including Avon Products and McDonald's, has helped Bath earn almost 13% annually over the past 10 years. During that period, Nationwide (800-848-0920) placed in the top 30% of growth and income funds while incurring 18% less volatility than the norm. Bath generates outsize gains with undersize risks by grabbing large-company growth stocks at reasonable prices. His fund's trailing 12-month PE of 23 is right in line with the S&P 500's. Yet five-year earnings growth was 16% higher than the market level. He isn't interested in a watered-down portfolio of hundreds of names. He currently has 40% of fund assets crammed into his 10 biggest holdings. "It's important to find an attractive situation and make it have an impact on the portfolio," says Bath. "I don't know what other managers are doing with so many stocks."

Investment Company of America.
The nine managers at ICA (800-421-4120) buy large-cap stocks that their research tells them are undervalued. The fund has weathered only 10 down years since its 1934 launch, the last back in 1977, when it dipped almost 3%. During the past 10 years, the ICA team has returned close to 13% annually while the fund registered 14% less volatility than the S&P 500. One way ICA has sidestepped calendar-year losses in the past 20 years is by loading up on dividend-paying stocks, such as Exxon and Bank of America. "We are part of a dying breed of growth and income managers who actually still pay attention to the income part of the equation," says ICA team member Jim Lovelace. Overall, ICA's 1.9% yield exceeds the 1.7% yield for the S&P 500. That's a claim fewer than 20% of growth and income funds can make. In some years, those dividend payouts make all the difference. In 1994, the value of the fund's stocks actually fell 2.4%. Thanks to the portfolio's income earnings of 2.6%, however, the fund eked out a 0.2% gain.

Dodge & Cox Balanced.
Its 10-person investment team generally keeps 60% of assets in large-cap stocks that appear undervalued relative to their earnings potential or asset value. The remaining 40% of Dodge & Cox Balanced (800-621-3979) is invested in high-quality corporate and government bonds. "We don't swing for the fences because we don't like the downside of doing that," says co-manager Harry Hagey, who has been with the firm for 30 years. The 65-year-old fund's somewhat stodgy approach has produced alluring results. Its 12% annualized gain during the past 10 years trails the all-stock S&P 500 by less than two percentage points, a remarkable feat considering the fund's 40% slug of bonds. The fund even excels when it loses. In 1981, its last negative year, the fund slid less than 3%, vs. a 5% drop in the S&P 500. The investing team, like that at ICA, looks for dividend-paying stocks. Financial stocks such as American Express and Citicorp account for about 20% of assets,

and another 20% is invested in cyclical smokestack stocks such as Dow Chemical and Deere. The ardent value investors have even managed to build a 13% stake in technology stocks, including Motorola and Hewlett-Packard, when they were temporarily out of favor.

Analytic Optioned Equity. Manager Chuck Dobson has led this fund on a winning streak by using various kinds of stock options to limit losses. One of his favorite ways to insulate Analytic (800-374-2633) from market downturns is by selling call options on some of his stock-holdings. Such sales generate steady income that acts as ballast during choppy markets. And indeed, Analytic's 10-year risk score is 40% below the level for the S&P 500. Note, however, that the income the fund gets from selling options creates big potential annual tax bills for shareholders. So the fund is best suited for tax-deferred retirement accounts. The trade-off for Analytic's dazzling defense is that the fund fields very little offensive firepower. In large part, that's a result of the options strategy. When stocks rise, the option buyer, not the fund, pockets the gains. Indeed, Analytic Optioned's close to 10% annualized return during the past 10 years trailed the S&P 500 by nearly four percentage points and ranks in the bottom third of growth and income funds.

Here's how Dobson himself sizes up the fund's prospects. He says his defensive tactics should keep the fund flat when the market declines 5%. Shareholders should experience just half the pain of S&P 500 indexers when the market is down more than 10%. The fund can keep pace in years when the S&P 500's total return is less than 8%. When stocks gain 8% to 20%, he expects the portfolio to collect about two-thirds of that advance. In years that the market soars more than 20%, he predicts his fund will get about half the market's return. "I don't think anyone should put all their money in this fund," says Dobson. "But if someone wants to sleep easy with 10% or so of their stock assets, then we make sense."

◆ TOP FOREIGN FUNDS TO CALL YOUR OWN

When you venture into overseas stock funds, it pays to stick with consistent winners that have a history of generating superior returns year after year. These stalwarts, as you might expect, aren't bull market belles. All have outperformed their peers in a variety of market conditions. To turn up these reliable performers we leaned heavily on Morningstar's fund ranking prowess. To start with, we had Morningstar calculate fund total returns for 85 rolling three-year periods. Many investment experts say that examining such overlapping periods gives a far more meaningful picture of a foreign fund's performance than its returns over the past three and five years. This method helps find funds that make their money steadily rather than in short, sharp bursts. Over time, you'll fare far better with such a Steady Eddie than with a fund that sizzles and then fizzles.

We initially selected two top choices. The first is **Euro Pacific Growth**, which boasts a 10-year Morningstar risk score 27% lower than the norm. Yet Euro Pacific produced a 10-year return of 13% annually. That landed the fund oceans ahead of the the Morgan Stanley EAFE index of stocks in the developed countries of Europe, Australasia and the Far East. Euro Pacific sustains its big gains by avoiding steep losses. In 1990, when the EAFE tumbled 23%, the fund broke even. When the EAFE slumped 12% in 1992, the fund rose 2%.

Euro Pacific is a member of the Capital Research and Management fund family, a Los Angeles group that has quietly carved out an enviable record of superb long-term, low-risk performance. Capital Research believes in team management and experience. Euro Pacific's six lead managers have a combined 120 years at the firm. "I've been here 14 years and I'm considered wet behind the ears," says Mark Denning, who shares frontline managerial duties with Thierry Vandeventer, Stephen Bepler, Robert Lovelace, Janet McKinley and Martial Chaillet. The portfolio is invested in more than two dozen countries, with 50% of assets in European nations and 11% in emerging markets such as Mexico and the Philippines. The fund's biggest country stake recently was its 11% commitment to Japan. "We're treading cautiously there," says Denning. "But we're finding some compelling individual stocks."

Investors who can tolerate steeper short-term swings may prefer **Ivy International A** managed by Hakan Castegran, a devout value investor. Ivy International's 10-year return of 13% annually has landed the portfolio in the top 25% of foreign funds in nine of the past 10 years. The fund is invested in around 20 countries, recently with 64% of assets in Europe, another 5% in Hong Kong and 15% in emerging markets including Russia.

We found ourselves in a bit of a quandary when it came to choosing a well-established fund that excels in the exotic and unpredictable arena of emerging markets. Only a handful of diversified emerging markets portfolios have five-year records, and only two of those stood out. Our favorite is **Merrill Lynch Developing Capital Markets** managed since 1989 by Grace Pineda. We're big fans of the fund's A shares, which carry a reasonable 1.4% annual expense ratio. But they are not available to retail investors. That leaves the B shares, which sport a pricey 2.8% expense ratio. That's a lot higher than we like. But Pineda's strong returns, and the lack of attractive alternatives, have led us to swallow hard and accept it.

Pineda and her team of analysts spend two months a year on the road visiting firms the world over. She is a value investor, looking for attractive companies whose stock prices don't yet reflect the intrinsic worth of their operations. Yet she isn't blind to the big picture. "Many times you can find a cheap stock that will just get cheaper if the macro-economics are not working for you," says Pineda. "So we pay attention to economic indicators such as world interest rates and trade balances." And her calls have been astute. The fund has returned 12% annually for the past five years. More than 25 countries are represented in the portfolio. Nearly 40% of fund assets recently were invested in Asian economies such as Malaysia's. Latin America accounted for another 27%.

◆ WHY BONDS MAY OUTPERFORM STOCKS

Bill Gross is regarded as one of the smartest bond fund managers of his generation. Yet Gross chooses a rather unflattering metaphor to describe fixed-income buyers. "Bond investors are the vampires of the investment world," he says. "They love decay, recession, anything that leads to low inflation." Inflation, of course, is the bane of the bond market because it drives up interest rates and thus drives down bond prices. Bond investors lately have been desperate for bad news. The economy has been growing steadily for six years, unemployment has declined since 1992 to below 5% and the consumer-confidence index has more than doubled. Not surprisingly, the S&P 500's 17% annual return over the period has lapped bonds' pedestrian 8.5% pace.

Gross says all this is about to change in the question-and-answer interview that follows. The manager of the Pimco funds argues that double-digit returns from stocks are coming to an end and that bonds figure to be more attractive for the next three years. Yet he reassures investors that they are not heading into the night of the living dead.

Q. What is the argument for buying bonds?

A. For starters, people have put so much in stocks already. A portfolio should balance the risk inherent in each security. But for many investors the teeter-totter is weighted all the way on the stock side. Sooner or later–and more likely sooner–there will be a correction in stocks. Investors will bear the full brunt of it.

Q. So is this a good time to buy bonds?

A. Absolutely! The best that I can forecast for stocks is an 8% total return. Dividends provide 2%, and the rest is earnings growth that you may or may not get. Bonds recently yielded a reliable 7%, with the possibility of something more if rates decline as I predict they will. That stacks up pretty well against stocks.

Q. What kind of stock market correction do you foresee?

A. I believe it will be less than 10%. Just think, stocks gained about that much in just the first two months of this year. But frankly, that's as much as they're going to gain all year. We've probably seen the peak. The correction will keep stocks flat for 1997 as a whole.

Q. So why not buy stocks on the next dip?

A. You won't get rewarded for it. At today's high prices, stock investors will have to adjust their sights to 6% annual average price appreciation over the next three years. That means they'll be waiting a lot longer to earn back money lost in dips.

Q. What will make your scenario come true?

A. The economy will grow more slowly at 1% to 2% a year, compared with the brisk 4% rate lately. This will happen as the strengthening dollar limits exports and consumers cut back on spending because they have already accumulated too much debt. Inflation will be lower, not higher, because oil prices are declining. And there's a flip side to the strong dollar. U.S. manufacturers, faced with more competition from imports, won't be able to raise prices.

Q. What about interest rates?

A. I see rates declining very gradually. The 30-year Treasury bond is yielding about 7%, and by year-end I think it will be close to 6.25%. True, Fed chairman Greenspan has raised short-term rates. But the economy will weaken. I think Greenspan will discover boosting rates was such a mistake that he will end up having to lower them again in 1998. Overall, I think we are in an environment in which long-term bonds will yield from 5% to 7%. The pressures of globalization will cap the upper end. The prime component of inflation is wages, and global competition is limiting wage increases. So interest rates can't go much higher than 7%. For them to fall below 5%, on the other hand, the economy would have to be running at zero inflation or deflation, which I don't think is a strong probability.

Q. How much of one's nest egg should be in bonds?

A. Allocations should be made according to a person's ability to stomach risk. For investors in their forties and fifties, I recommend an overall split of 70% in stocks and 30% in bonds. I'd break down the bond portion as follows: 40% in Treasuries that mature in five to 10 years, 25% in corporate debt of the same maturities, 25% in mortgage-backed securities like Ginnie Maes and Fannie Maes and 10% in foreign government issues. I think inflation is going to cool. If you don't and want to protect yourself against it, you could put the whole 30% into the new inflation-indexed Treasury bonds. They're the deodorants of the bond world. They take the worry out of your day. These bonds not only are guaranteed against default. They also promise that you'll always earn a rate of interest above the rate of inflation. Right now, they're paying a 3.3% return after inflation. That's attractive for such a secure investment.

Q. Why put only 30% of your portfolio in bonds?

A. Over the long term, stocks return more than bonds. That said, however, I would suggest 50% in bonds and 50% in stocks for the rest of 1997. If stock prices have peaked as I think they have, the only money investors will see is 2% from dividends. You can earn three times that in bonds.

Q. Should investors buy individual bonds?

A. If you have less than six figures to invest, buy funds. The things to consider before you invest are the return, obviously, but also fees and maturity. When you're looking at single-digit returns, fees can take a big chunk out of your income. So don't pay any more than 0.5%. Extend your maturities to pick up additional yield. If you are already in a bond fund with a five-year maturity, switch to one maturing in seven to eight years. And if you have a 10-year average maturity, then go out to 13 or 14 years. If you've never invested in bonds, take the money you have in a money-market or savings account and put it in a short-term fund that invests in notes going out only two to three years. You won't add much risk, and you'll earn 1.5 percentage points more than you'd get in a money market.

Q. Why do you like mortgage-backed bonds so much?
A. They are usually rated AAA or AA and have implicit government protection against default. Plus their yields ranging from 7.5% to 8% are very attractive with inflation at 2% to 3%. I'd recommend buying them in a fund like Vanguard Fixed Income GNMA. Vanguard has the lowest fees in the industry and is well managed. Pimco is close on fees. But we don't have a Ginnie Mae fund.

Q. What kind of foreign bonds do you recommend?
A. Put your money in emerging market bond funds. Here's why. Many international funds are not completely hedged in U.S. dollars. So when the dollar is as strong as it is now, the unhedged funds suffer currency losses. But emerging market bond funds are primarily invested in dollar-denominated Brady bonds. So there's much less currency risk with these funds. Moreover, they hold South American or Eastern European bonds yielding 9% to 10%, while German bonds pay 5.5% and Japanese only 2.5%. I like Scudder Emerging Markets Income and have even put members of my own family in it.

◆ YOUR BEST INVESTMENTS FOR INCOME

To help you diversify your retirement holdings, here's our rundown of the most appealing investments for generating reliable income including both individual securities and mutual funds that hold them. You should plan to keep the investments for a year or longer. And don't panic if interest rates rise a little later this year. They are likely to come back down by the middle of next year.

U.S. Government bonds. Investors seeking dependable income with no risk of default need look no further than Treasury bonds. The interest on Treasuries is exempt from both state and local taxes, which can add the equivalent of half a percentage point to the yield for top-bracket investors in high-tax states. Fund investors might want to consider **Vanguard Fixed–Income Intermediate U.S. Treasury**, which has an average seven-year maturity and attractive 6.3% yield.

Treasury STRIPS, also known as zero-coupon bonds, pay no annual cash interest during their lifetime. Instead, holders receive a lump sum at maturity that includes interest accrued over the bond's life. This structure eliminates the need to reinvest your interest. So you know both your annual rate of return and the exact value of your investment at maturity. Since zeros are extremely sensitive to rate changes, they capture the biggest capital gains if rates decline. For instance, if yields on zeros fall to 6% over the next year, 20-year zeros would return 34%. Fund investors can choose among zero-bond portfolios with a variety of maturities like **American Century–Benham Target Maturities Trust 2005, Target Maturities 2010 and Target Maturities 2015**.

What about the inflation-indexed Treasuries that were introduced in January 1997? These 10-year notes are specifically designed to protect investors from the ravages of rising prices. Thus their principal and interest are adjusted every six months to reflect the going inflation rate. Inflation-indexed notes, which have many of the characteristics of zero-coupon bonds, make the most sense for an investor who's still saving for retirement within a tax-deferred 401(k) plan or IRA.

Tax-free municipal bonds. Depending on your tax bracket, municipal bonds may offer juicier after-tax yields than Treasuries of comparable maturities. Topnotch 15-year munis recently paid 5.5%, equivalent to a taxable yield of 7.6% for investors in the 28% tax bracket. That's nine-tenths of a percentage point more than 15-year Treasuries yielded. Stick to bonds rated double A or higher by two rating agencies, such as Moody's or Standard & Poor's. James Cooner of the Bank of New York's tax-exempt bond division recommends financially sound states' general-obligation bonds as well as issues backed by water or sewer revenues. "The latter are monopolistic services that people can't avoid using," he notes. But if you don't have $100,000 or so to spread across four or five individual munis, Cooner suggests that you invest instead in a mutual fund and pay close attention to the portfolio's average maturity. Analyst Wright recommends **Vanguard**

Municipal Intermediate. The fund's portfolio of munis with intermediate maturities averaging eight years recently yielded 5%. That's the taxable equivalent of 6.9% for investors in the 28% bracket.

Convertible bonds and preferred stock. These securities
share in most of a common stock's upside but not as much of its downside. "If you think stocks are overpriced, convertibles are a great way to be cautious," says Ted Southworth, manager of the **Northern Income Equity** fund. That's because until a convert is exchanged for the company's common, or until the convert matures or is redeemed, it acts partly like a bond and produces regular income. That can cushion your portfolio when stock prices fall. Note that most convertible bonds are not actively traded on exchanges. So you might instead invest in them through a top-ranked fund such as Northern Income. You can buy many convertible preferred shares on an exchange in round lots of 100 shares. Neil Feinberg, co-manager of the Mainstay Convertible Fund, likes **Microsoft Preferred** (traded over the counter, around $81; 2.8% yield). With a guaranteed minimum payment of $80 when the preferred matures in 1999, it will deliver a 12% compound annual return if Microsoft's common stock reaches Feinberg's $120 target price by then.

Real estate investment trusts. REITs, which own and man-
age offices, stores, apartments or other properties, offer a solid 6% average yield. Because of that hefty payout, REIT prices are only about half as volatile as those of other stocks. Rising real estate prices in most parts of the country mean that REITs' rents and earnings are generally on the upswing. Many analysts recommend hotel, industrial and office REITs rather than those that concentrate on residential properties. "Office and industrial complexes are renegotiating leases written during the real estate recession of the late 1980s and early 1990s, so market rents are rising," says analyst Cathy Creswell of brokerage Alex. Brown & Sons in Baltimore. Barry Curtis, also of Alex. Brown, likes **Bradley Real Estate** (NYSE, around $19; 6.9% yield). He predicts that this retail REIT's neighborhood shopping centers will help fuel earnings growth of 7.5% annually through the year 2000. Fund investors might consider **Cohen & Steers Realty Shares**. Almost 50% of its assets are invested in offices and regional malls, which paid off handsomely last year as increasing occupancy rates forced up rents. The fund has returned 20% annually over the past five years.

3

HOW TO

CREATE A

COZY NEST EGG

The perfect investment for retirement offers terrific long-term gains, bountiful dividends and never, ever loses money. Alas, such a paragon doesn't exist. No stock, bond or fund can deliver both high returns and safety. Investing always means weighing potential benefits against risks (see the box "Prepare for These Investing Pitfalls" on page 56). The cardinal rule is that the more safety you demand, the less return you can expect, and vice versa. That means you cannot search intelligently for the best investments without some soul searching first. These questions will help you define what's best for you.

Is growth, income or safety paramount? You're a growth

investor if your key need is to build capital for a major expense, such as your kids' college education or your own retirement, that's five or more years away. The best investments for you aim mainly for capital appreciation. Such stocks and funds have a strong record of appreciation over long periods but are also the most prone to harsh short-term setbacks. As a result, you shouldn't consider yourself a growth investor unless you can endure painful stretches when your portfolio is down 20% or more. If you want your portfolio to help you pay ongoing expenses, such as your living costs in retirement, you're an income investor. Look at bonds, stocks and funds sporting above-average yields. If you need money for an expense you will incur within a few years, what you need from your investments is safety. Your best choices are ultrasafe money-market funds. The drawback is that their yields have been achingly low in recent years.

How much risk can you handle? Think of risk as the entry

fee you pay to invest. You can choose to take a lot or a little. But you can never avoid it entirely. The payback for assuming more risk is potential return. The most aggressive stock funds, for example, have suffered precipitous falls of 20% or so in their worst years. But their long-term returns lately averaged close to 13% annually. Thus risk isn't necessarily bad if you don't take on more than you can stomach.

When will you need the money? The longer you're planning to hold on to your investments, the more you can afford to shoot for the stock market's higher returns. Say you had invested in the S&P 500 index at the start of any calendar year in the past 55 years and pulled out after 12 months. According to the research firm Ibbotson Associates, you would have made money two out of three times. Had you held on for five years, your odds of making a profit would have improved to four out of five. And if you stood by your stocks for 10 years, you would have finished in the black 96% of the time.

How much could you bear to lose? No matter how impressive a stock's or fund's long-term record may be, you won't score big if you bail out when the performance turns temporarily cold. So ask yourself how much you could stand to see your investment plunge in a given year before pulling the ripcord. If you're willing to weather losses of 10% or more in a year, you're an aggressive investor. That suits you for high-risk, high-return stocks and aggressive growth funds. A 5% threshold suggests you're interested in trading off some performance for safety in, say, total return funds that blend high-yielding stocks and bonds. If you're unwilling to tolerate any losses, you're too conservative for virtually any stock fund and all but the safest bond portfolios. Your options are money-market funds or those invested in government bonds of short or intermediate maturities.

◆ LOOK FOR YOUR PORTFOLIO'S BLIND SPOTS

To identify potential hazards in your investment strategy, fill out the worksheet "Rate Your Retirement Portfolio's Risk" beginning on page 58. Then decide how to redeploy assets to reduce your exposure. Don't limit your inventory to investments that are kept in your brokerage account. Your earning power probably is by far your most valuable asset; equity in a home may come next. Many investors also have sub-

◆ Prepare for These Investing Pitfalls

Regardless of your age or how well you have diversified your retirement portfolio, the most important challenge is to find your comfort zone and to know that it will change as your temples gray and your career progresses. Astute asset allocation begins with a careful analysis of your investments and other aspects of your financial life to see how each of these affects your exposure to the following types of risk.

◆ **Inflation risk.** Rising prices will reduce the purchasing power of an investment. An annual inflation rate of 5% over 15 years will cut the value of $1,000 to $480. Overcautious investors who hoard assets in money-market funds may not earn enough to outpace rising prices. Rising inflation also erodes the value of future income generated by investments with fixed payments, most notably long-term bonds.

◆ **Interest rate risk.** Rising rates will cause investments to drop in price. Higher rates make yields on existing bonds less attractive, so their market values decline. Rising rates also hurt stocks by making their dividend yields less appealing. People who invest borrowed money through margin accounts or have other types of floating-rate debt increase their risk because higher interest rates cut into their net profits.

◆ **Economic risk.** Slower growth in the economy will cause investments to fall in price. Shares of small growth companies may shrink because they require a booming economy to sustain their robust earnings gains. Cyclical companies, such as automakers and chemical producers, can't easily cut their hefty fixed costs during a recession. So their earnings and share prices may well nosedive. Economic downturns can also undercut junk bonds issued by financially weak firms that might default.

◆ **Market risk.** This includes such factors as political developments and Wall Street fads that can batter investment markets. Tax law changes, trade agreements, program trading and the quirks of investor psychology all contribute to market risk, which has accounted for much of the stock market's day-to-day volatility. Gold also carries considerable market risk because its price moves sharply when political or military upheavals in other countries encourage the flight of capital.

◆ **Specific risk.** This covers occurrences that may affect only a particular company or industry. Poor management or bad luck can dampen earnings or even bankrupt a company. And high-flying growth stocks are particularly vulnerable to earnings disappointments. Individuals take on a high degree of specific risk when they buy stock in a firm with a heavy debt burden or invest in specialty stock funds, often called sector funds, that concentrate their holdings in a single field such as healthcare providers or high-technology companies. Specific risk also includes the chance that sudden changes in government regulation will harm a particular group of companies.

stantial assets invested in company pension plans or insurance policies with significant cash values. And entrepreneurs should take a close reading of the risks that threaten the value of their small business.

Risk can creep up on even vigilant fund investors. Your holdings in a retirement plan may grow more quickly than you realize, particularly if you make regular contributions or reinvest your returns. Growth in one asset can throw a portfolio out of balance if other investments don't keep up. If a prolonged bull market boosts the value of your stock funds, you may need to sell some shares to restore the balance between stocks and other assets. Similarly, when a single fund does extremely well, you have to consider whether it's time to shed some shares. Be especially wary of loading up on your company's stock through savings plans sponsored by your firm. If the company runs into trouble, both your job and your stock could be endangered at the same time. To gauge your own situation, you will need to conduct a survey of your investments and other aspects of your finances.

Stocks and stock funds. They are vulnerable to the possibility that skittish investors will panic for some reason and drive share prices down en masse (that's an example of market risk). But risks related to inflation, interest rates or economic growth may vary considerably. For example, a sharp increase in the inflation rate depresses stock prices because it may reduce the purchasing power of future dividends to shareholders. What's more, inflation generally coincides with higher interest rates, which draw investors from stocks to bonds. Because firms such as retailers, consumer product manufacturers and service companies can more readily pass along cost increases to customers, they have a better chance to prosper during periods of high inflation. Slowing economic growth hurts some firms more than others. Manufacturers with high overhead, known as cyclicals, cannot easily cut costs when a recession slices sales. So their earnings can quickly tail off. Many small growth companies also require an expanding economy to sustain their earnings growth and stock prices. By contrast, firms that sell necessities such as food or clothing often shine even in a lackluster economy. Since overseas stocks are partly immune to changes in the American economy and markets, they may stand firm while U.S. stocks sink. Unlike domestic issues, however, foreign shares carry currency risk. A weaker dollar abroad helps to inflate returns earned by American investors on overseas assets, while a stronger dollar deflates them.

◆ Rate Your Retirement Portfolio's Risk

Most people shield some of their fund investments against different types of risk. But few balance all of their assets so that they are well protected. This quiz can help you identify your points of vulnerability. With each question, you will accumulate points for one or more of the five major investment risks that are described in the main text. Write the points in the boxes below. Then total the points for each risk and interpret your scores as follows. Fewer than five points is low. Five to 10 points is moderate. Above 10 points is high. While you may want to vary your exposure to different categories of risk, depending on your personal circumstances and outlook for the financial markets, any score that comes in above 10 points should set off alarm bells.

Once you have identified vulnerabilities, you can take steps to shore up your defenses. Say that you score high for inflation risk and low for market risk. You might balance your portfolio better by switching some cash from money-market funds to those invested in stocks or gold-mining shares. While your risk of a temporary decline in the value of your portfolio will increase, you will have a better chance of outpacing inflation.

In answering the questions, don't make the mistake of overlooking funds located in 401(k) accounts, IRAs or any other savings or deferred-compensation plans. It may be difficult to pin down the value of some assets. For instance, you may have a universal life policy with an important investment component. Just make the best estimates that you can. It isn't necessary to be exact. But it is important that your inventory be as complete as possible.

Questions

	INFLATION RISK	INTEREST RATE RISK	ECONOMIC RISK	MARKET RISK	SPECIFIC RISK
◆ Are your assets diversified among fewer than four of these five categories—stocks, real estate, gold, bonds and cash? If yes, score one point for each risk.					
◆ Are more than 35% of your assets invested in any one of the five categories? If yes, score one point for each risk.					
◆ Is at least 10% of your portfolio in assets such as gold, natural-resource stocks or high-grade collectibles such as rare stamps? If no, score one point for inflation risk.					
◆ Is at least 30% of your portfolio in investments such as growth stocks and real estate, which are likely to produce long-term capital gains that can outpace inflation? If no, score two points for inflation risk.					
◆ Are your real estate and gold investments held primarily in assets such as gold-mining shares and REITs (real estate investment trusts), which tend to fluctuate with the stock market? If yes, score one point for market risk.					
◆ Do you generally keep at least 15% of your portfolio in cash equivalents such as Treasury bills or money-market funds? If no, score two points for interest rate risk.					
◆ Is more than 30% of your portfolio composed of assets such as long-term government bonds, CDs (certificates of deposit) or annuities that promise to pay investors fixed payments over a period of many years? If yes, then score three points each for inflation and interest rate risk.					

	INFLATION RISK	INTEREST RATE RISK	ECONOMIC RISK	MARKET RISK	SPECIFIC RISK
◆ Do highly volatile zero-coupon bonds account for more than 30% of your fixed-income assets? If yes, score two points each for inflation and interest rate risk.					
◆ Do small growth stocks or junk bonds, which may fall sharply in a recession, account for more than 25% of your portfolio? If yes, score three points for economic risk.					
◆ Do you switch money among different assets to try and catch the highs and lows of different investment markets? If yes, score two points for market risk.					
◆ Do you use dollar cost averaging or a similar plan that involves adding money to your investment portfolio at regular intervals? If no, score two points for market risk.					
◆ Is more than 20% of your portfolio concentrated in a single industry? If yes, score three points each for economic risk, market risk and specific risk.					
◆ Do stocks or bonds issued by one company (including the one that you work for) or shares in a single mutual fund or limited partnership account for more than 15% of your assets? If yes, score three points each for economic risk, market risk and specific risk.					
◆ Does your share in a privately held business account for more than 30% of your portfolio? If yes, score one point for economic risk and four points for specific risk.					
◆ Does a rental property account for more than 30% of your portfolio? If yes, score one point for economic risk and three points for specific risk.					
◆ Do foreign stocks and shares of domestic companies with significant overseas sales account for less than 10% of your portfolio? If yes, score one point for economic risk.					
◆ Will you need access in the next three to five years to principal in volatile assets such as stocks or long-term bonds? If yes, score one point each for inflation, interest rate, economic and market risk.					
◆ Do you have variable-rate loans such as mortgages or credit-card revolving debt that recently has amounted to 30% or more of the market value of your portfolio? If yes, score four points for interest rate risk.					
◆ Is 20% or more of your portfolio financed by loans or invested in highly leveraged assets such as options? If yes, score one point each for interest rate and market risk.					
TOTAL					

Bonds and bond funds. Their prices fall when interest rates rise. But the extent of the drop depends on a bond's maturity and the amount of its coupon. Short-term bonds fall slightly when interest rates move upward, and a high coupon also offers some protection against climbing rates. At the opposite extreme, zero-coupon bonds fall sharply when rates head higher. A recession generally brings lower interest rates, which boost bond prices. But some issues react negatively to the threat of an economic slowdown. So-called junk bonds, in particular, may lose ground because investors fear that financially weak firms will default and fail to make payments of interest and principal to bondholders on time. U.S. Treasury and high-grade corporate bonds gain the most during hard times because income investors seek them out as safe havens.

Real estate investments. Although properties tend to keep pace with inflation over time, they present other hazards. If you own a rental property, you run the risk that you won't find a tenant. A real estate partnership that owns several properties in different regions can reduce such risks through diversification. But it may lose value if tax changes or a recession drive down property values across the country. Real estate investment trusts, called REITs, and the funds that own them, can fluctuate with the stock market as well as with property values.

Gold and other hard assets. Both bullion and gold-mining stocks have been lackluster over the past decade of generally low inflation. But the price of gold can skyrocket when the inflation rate rises rapidly. Between 1968 and 1988, the consumer price index posted nine annual spurts of 6% or more. During that time frame, gold rewarded investors with gains averaging 34% annually. Gold stocks and the funds that own them are more volatile than the metal itself. A miners' strike might boost the price of bullion but cut profits at mining companies. Other tangible assets such as antiques present their own problems.

◆ GET IN SYNC WITH THE BUSINESS CYCLE

You understand that when interest rates rise, stocks and bonds suffer, and when the economy stops growing, eventually your portfolio does too. But buried under all the economic statistics in your newspaper is a potentially more profitable insight—where we stand in the business cycle.

That's the term used to describe the economy's never-ending shuttle between expansion and contraction. Not surprisingly, the cycle and the stock market's performance are inextricably linked. "As much as 60% of a stock's price movements can be attributed to the business cycle," explains Sam Stovall at Standard & Poor's in New York City. "The cycle dominates both the direction of the overall market and the fortunes of individual industry groups." A study by Jeremy Siegel, a professor of finance at the Wharton School of Business, found that an investor who managed to anticipate every turn in the business cycle since World War II would have outperformed a buy-and-hold stock owner by up to 4.8 percentage points a year over two decades. That's the difference between turning $10,000 into $86,600 and turning it into $201,400.

The economy is making headlines now that it's in the sixth year of a growth phase that began in March 1991, the third longest expansion in postwar history. Expansions average about four years, with the full cycle typically lasting just five. The unusually long run of fat years suggests to many market analysts that the economy is now overdue for a shrinking spell, as discussed in Chapter 2. If that forecast is correct, the stock market is likely to sell off beforehand. Indeed, MONEY sees a 15% to 20% drop within 12 months.

Turning points of a cycle tend to be clear only in hindsight, of course. Economists always disagree on where we are at present in the cycle, let alone where we're headed. So let's be clear. Understanding the business cycle won't allow you to match Siegel's hypothetical investor and switch all your money between stocks and bonds at precisely the right moment. But it can signal you to make modest adjustments to your portfolio, which in the long run will boost your returns. Equally important, monitoring the cycle can help you avoid emotional mistakes. To understand why, look at how a typical business cycle unfolds. It has five phases—an early, middle and late expansion followed by an early and late contraction. Each of the nine cycles since World War II has left stock prices higher than before. But stocks in certain industries outperform others during each phase.

Early expansion. It lasts an average of 17 months and is the best time to own stocks. That's when falling interest rates, lower inflation and the anticipation of improved corporate profits combine to push share prices higher. The S&P 500 index typically gains an average of 22% in this phase. But stocks in the top-performing industries, such as transportation and technology, can soar 30% to 45% because their sales quickly reflect any pickup in economic activity.

Middle expansion. It also lasts an average of 17 months during which rising consumer demand eventually encourages companies to build new plants and hire more workers. So investors switch their attention to capital-goods companies, such as manufacturing and construction, and service businesses, such as those that supply temporary office workers. The stock market typically climbs 12% overall.

Late expansion. It plants the seeds of the next contraction in the cycle. Consumer spending and industrial production slow down, while inflation and interest rates rise. The market typically turns choppy and edges up just 9% or so over a period that averages about 17 months. Corporations reduce their purchases to essential goods and services. So the best returns tend to go to companies that provide basic industrial materials, such as aluminum, chemicals or energy.

Early contraction. Rising interest rates eventually choke off growth. Consumer expectations plunge, unemployment rises and industrial production drops off. This early contraction phase typically lasts six months. If GDP (gross domestic product) drops for two successive quarters, it's officially a recession. Scared investors flock to consumer staple stocks, such as food and drug companies and utilities, which promise steady returns even in a sluggish economy. Overall, stocks tend to fall 10% on average.

Late contraction. For an average of about six months, consumer expectations begin to revive, the decline in industrial production slows, inflation is flat, and interest rates fall. Interest-sensitive stocks, including those in the financial sector and automaking, start to outpace stocks in other industries. The market as a whole moves up an average of 8% as investors anticipate the start of the next expansion.

The market doesn't move simultaneously with the economy. Stock prices reflect investors' expectations for future earnings, not just current profits. That's why the most profitable time to move is several months before a new economic phase begins. For example, over past business cycles, the stock market has typically begun to surge about five months before the start of an expansion and begun to slump about seven months ahead of a contraction. Investors' fears of losing their gains apparently outweigh their greed. Remember too that business cycles rarely follow the textbook pattern. Outside factors can lengthen, shorten or otherwise distort them. The biggest influence comes from the Federal Reserve, which attempts to minimize the swings of the business cycle by raising or lowering interest rates. For example, in 1994, Fed chairman Alan Greenspan hiked rates a total of seven times in order to cool the economy and prevent a resurgence of inflation. If the Fed is successful, economic growth slows just enough to allow the business cycle to expand once again, without the pain of recession.

Where we are in the cycle now. Forecasters agree that the early part of the expansion is behind us and so are the biggest market gains. The multimillion-dollar question is how close is the next contraction? Most forecasters believe that the economy will continue to boom in 1997. "This expansion is chronologically old. But it behaves as if it's much younger," says economist Allen Sinai of Primark Decision Economics in New York City. "We have stable interest rates, a strong bull market and no serious economic imbalances." Others think the economy will start retrenching soon. "Corporate profits are starting to suffer because consumer demand is slowing, and companies are under tremendous pressure not to raise their prices," notes economist David Bostian at brokerage Herzog Heine Geduld in New York City. "Investors are punishing stocks severely for failing to meet expectations." Bostian says a recession is likely this year and could be preceded by a market correction of as much as 15%.

One thing is clear no matter whom you believe. You shouldn't wait until the next phase begins to position your portfolio because the market will have moved before you. Now's the time to adjust your strategy for a period of slower growth. Within the portion of your portfolio that's allotted to individual stocks, increase your holdings of energy and defensive consumer staple stocks, such as healthcare companies. Fund investors might want to take some profits in their aggressive growth portfolios and shift that money into less risky growth and income holdings. Oppenheimer & Co. strategist Michael Metz also suggests buying companies with strong overseas sales, such as drug manufacturers. "Although we are looking for an economic slowdown in the U.S.," he says, "foreign economies are accelerating, especially in Europe and

Lapses in judgment are not the only reasons why you may slip up in your retirement planning. You can also trip up simply when you don't know enough about certain financial matters. This test was designed to measure your grasp of the fundamentals of investing, credit, taxes and insurance. Give yourself 10 points for each correct answer (explained in the box at right).

1. Since 1926, which of the following types of investments overwhelmingly earned more than the other two?
a) Stocks
b) Long-term U.S. Government bonds
c) Short-term Treasury bills

2. Over the past 25 years, which of these investment strategies was the least likely to experience wild swings in value?
a) 100% long-term U.S. Government bonds
b) 70% large-company U.S. stocks and 30% intermediate-term U.S. Government bonds
c) 70% large-company U.S. stocks and 30% small-company U.S. stocks

3. When interest rates rise, bond prices
a) Rise
b) Fall
c) Neither. Interest-rate moves do not directly affect bond prices.

4. You invest $1,000 in a stock. After one year, the stock price falls 20%. The next year, the price jumps 20%. After those two years, you have
a) Broken even
b) Made money
c) Lost money

5. When selecting a mutual fund, it is most important that you
a) Evaluate the fund's five-year performance record.
b) Pick a fund that meets your investment goals.
c) Pick a fund whose manager is well-respected.
d) Pick a fund with low fees.

6. It is safer to buy a mutual fund from a bank than from a brokerage firm.
True or false?

7. You cannot lose money that you invest in a money-market fund.
True or false?

8. Any wage earner under age 70.5 can contribute some money to an IRA.
True or false?

9. Interest on a home-equity line of credit is tax deductible
a) Always
b) Sometimes
c) Never

10. Who pays the federal gift tax incurred on gifts of more than $10,000?
a) The giver
b) The person receiving the gift

11. U.S. consumers owe an average of $3,300 in credit-card debt. Assuming 17.7% annual interest charges, how long would it take you to pay off that balance if you paid only the minimum monthly payments?
a) Four years
b) Seven years
c) 12 years
d) 19 years

12. Which of these life insurance products is best if you want the largest immediate death benefit for the lowest premium?
a) Whole life
b) Term
c) Universal life
d) Variable life

Answers

1. a. Stocks have returned roughly 11% annually since 1926, vs. 5% for bonds and 3.7% for T-bills.

2. b. The portfolio of U.S. stocks and bonds was about one-third less volatile than U.S. bonds alone and half as volatile as the mix of small- and large-company U.S. stocks.

3. b.

4. c. To make up your loss you would need a 25% gain.

5. b.

6. False. Unlike bank deposits, mutual funds sold through banks are not insured.

7. False. Money-market funds are not guaranteed, though no individual investor has ever lost money in one because fund companies have so far made up for any shortfalls.

8. True, though not everyone can deduct their contributions from their income taxes. Those who can deduct include taxpayers who do not have qualified retirement plans at work or anyone who earns less than $25,000 a year (less than $40,000 for married couples).

9. b. Interest on home-equity loans is tax deductible for up to $100,000 of the loan.

10. a. The giver pays federal taxes on any gift to an individual that exceeds $10,000 in one year. Tip: you can give the gift of college tuition or medical expenses of any amount tax-free so long as the money is paid directly to the appropriate institution.

11. d. Paying only $10 a month more will shorten that period to four years.

12. b. Note, however, that term policies pay only a basic death benefit. Whole life and universal life policies build cash value in addition to the death benefit. Variable life pays a death benefit and allows you to direct the premiums into stock and bond investment accounts.

Scoring

120: Congratulations! You're a personal finance whiz. **90 to 110:** Very knowledgeable. You have a good grip on your finances. Now you just have to watch those mental lapses. **50 to 80:** Not bad. But you are vulnerable to some basic blunders. **40 or less:** Start cramming.

Japan. Whether you should trim your stock holdings overall depends primarily on your financial goals, time horizon and risk tolerance. But it makes sense to cut your exposure to stocks in favor of fixed income if you expect to need your money for retirement within five years or so.

◆ INVESTING FOR LONG-TERM GROWTH

History suggests that stocks return about 2.7 times as much as do money-market funds and twice as much as bonds in the long term. But from one month or one year to the next you can lose serious money in the stock market. The possibility of short-term losses is a constant in today's skittish market. So a prudent investor will take some elementary precautions. For starters, don't consider investing in stock or stock funds unless you're reasonably sure you won't need the money within five years. That's roughly the length of the typical economic cycle. If you were unlucky enough to put your money in at a market peak, you may need the full cycle to recover your losses and make a profit. If you suffer a 30% loss in your first year of investing, it would take you almost four years at a 10% annual return to get even. The best way to avoid such unfortunate timing is to ease into the market gradually by making equal payments over a matter of months or years, regardless of whether stocks are rising or falling.

More and more investors whose goal is growth are focusing on fund managers' investment styles for the simple reason that people differ on what makes a stock appealing. By training or temperament, managers gravitate toward stocks with certain traits. Some favor those of small companies (market values under $1 billion). Others like large blue-chip firms. And still others prefer companies in the middle called mid-caps. Within those sizes, managers may seek either fast-growing firms or seeming bargains. Learning where your fund fits in is more than just pigeonholing. Academic studies show that style accounts for at least 75% of a typical growth fund's return.

Small vs. large companies. Each of these two approaches has its own investment logic and its own roster of successful practitioners. Small-cap or mid-cap fund managers specialize in those companies on the theory that young, entrepreneurial firms have the most explosive growth potential. The risk, however, is that small-stock funds are prone to unpredictable downturns that can swiftly wipe out 10% to 20% of their value. Other managers prefer the stocks of corporate giants. The argument for them is that they are Wall Street's best source of stable profits. The problem is that it's hard for even the shrewdest managers to uncover hidden opportunities among the most widely followed stocks.

Growth vs. value approach. After size, the primary style distinction is between so-called growth and value investors. The former want to own the fastest growing, most successful companies (e.g., the Microsofts, Wal-Marts, Home Depots and their successors) capable of expanding their earnings a brisk 15% or better a year. The problem is that such premium companies usually trade at rich prices relative to their earnings. Thus their stocks can fall hard in the event that earnings fail to live up to investors' lofty expectations. Value managers are the stock market's equivalent of flea market browsers. They're looking for cast-aside stocks trading at prices that may not reflect the true value of their assets or future earnings. How do you discern a manager's style? For size distinctions, simply call the fund sponsor and ask for the fund's median market capitalization, or the total market value of the fund's median stock. To tell whether the manager is a growth getter or value seeker, look at the fund's yield and price-earnings ratio (calculated by references like Morningstar). A value fund generally will have a higher than average yield and a lower than average PE. A growth fund will be the opposite.

Which size or style is best? Research suggests that over the long haul, small-company stocks tend to beat out big ones, and value stocks have the edge over growth. For example, Trinity Investment Management based in Cambridge, Mass. studied growth vs. value stocks over a 24-year stretch and found that value won, returning 12% annually relative to growth's 9%. Here's one rationale. Because value stocks by definition already trade at depressed prices, they tend to fall less far in bear markets. In the five losing markets included in the Trinity study, value stocks dropped an average of about 17%, while the typical growth stock lost 25%. As for small-caps, Trinity's calculations show that these stocks edged out large companies by nearly one percentage point a year (or 10.4% to 9.6%). Over shorter time spans, however, it's a much tighter race in which each of the different styles takes its turn in the lead for periods that generally last two to five years.

Trying to predict precisely when the cycle is going to shift is as futile as any other kind of market timing. That's why choosing among investment styles is primarily a tool of diversification. By owning stock funds of every style, you can effectively smooth out the inevitable ups and downs of Wall Street fashions. Just as important, you'll be able to distinguish between fund managers whose performance is lagging merely because their investment approach is currently out of vogue and those who simply have lost their touch.

◆ BROADENING YOUR HORIZONS ABROAD

Foreign stock funds are ideal if you lack the resolve to become fluent in faraway markets. There are four subcategories based upon breadth of investing focus. The broadest are global funds, which can invest anywhere in the world including the U.S., followed by international funds, which invest everywhere in the world except the U.S. Then there are regional funds, which invest in a specific segment of the globe such as Latin America, and single-country funds. Investors first beginning to diversify worldwide can probably cut through the confusion of choices by ignoring global and single-country funds and zeroing in on internationals. Why? The problem with global funds is that the manager's freedom to acquire U.S. stocks can negate your whole purpose of buying the fund–to diversify overseas. The typical global fund today puts some 40% of its assets in the U.S. Thus if you're aiming to reallocate a portfolio mix to contain, say, one-quarter holdings abroad, you could calibrate that percentage more precisely with an international fund, a pure overseas play. And investors often find single-country funds too risky, narrowly focused or both.

For many small investors, funds are often the only viable vehicles for venturing into uncharted international waters. Most foreign stock markets do not impose reporting standards on companies that are as stringent as those enforced by government regulators here. So such financial information is not only harder to obtain but also tends to be less reliable. Worse, buying foreign securities exposes you to two special types of risk. The first is political risk, or the danger that unexpected electoral shifts or governmental instability will adversely affect a market. For example, shares in the closed-end Mexico Fund tumbled following the assassination of the leading presidential candidate. The other worry commonly looming over foreign investing is currency risk. This is the danger that the value of the U.S. dollar abroad will rise and thereby shrink your returns overseas.

Suppose you take $1,000 and convert it into Japanese yen at a time when the dollar is worth 100 yen. Then you spend those 100,000 yen on 100 shares of a Japanese stock fund at 1,000 yen per share. What would happen if the dollar rises in value to 125 yen but your fund goes nowhere? If you decided to bail out, you would get the same price you paid (100,000 yen) but net out only $800 after converting your proceeds back into dollars (100,000 divided by 125). So you lost 20% (not counting brokerage commissions) on your investment even though your Japanese fund held firm. Of course, if the dollar fell the same percent against the yen, you would have profited 20% on that stagnant fund. The reassuring news is that the dollar's currency swings tend to cancel each other out over the long term, leaving no significant statistical impact on portfolio performance. But the short-term currency threat may rule out the notion of international diversification for some conservative investors.

◆ AIMING FOR INCOME AND GROWTH

Reflect on the fact that 75% of bond fund investors don't spend a penny of the income that their funds produce. Instead, they reinvest their payout in more fund shares, suggesting many mistakenly use bond funds as tools for capital growth. Yet the bond market's historic return is only about half that of stocks. In other words, if you rely entirely on bonds to meet your long-range financial goals, you risk coming up short. What about bonds' reputation for lower risk? Well, it's generally true, but not always. As interest rates zigzagged through the 1980s, long-term corporate and government bonds were nearly 20% more volatile than was the S&P 500 index. Then you have to factor in the pernicious effect of inflation. Looking back at all the five-year periods since 1937, the stocks in the S&P 500 index beat inflation by an average of 7.3 percentage points annually. But intermediate-term Treasury bonds (those maturing in five to 10 years) nosed out rising prices by just one percentage point.

If you have financial goals more than five years off, take a deep breath and admit that at least some of your money belongs in stocks.

That doesn't mean you have to dive into the deep end of the market where the aggressive growth funds swim, however. Instead, wade into total return funds, a moderate-risk category embracing such major subsets as equity income and balanced portfolios. Some seek capital gains as a secondary goal by supplementing their bond holdings with high-dividend stocks or convertible securities. Convertibles are essentially hybrids (issued either as bonds or preferred stock) that pay fixed income the same way that bonds do but can be exchanged for shares of the issuing company's common stock at a specified price. Total return funds aim to blend the bondlike attributes of steady income with stocklike spurts of capital appreciation. That has allowed them to grow several percentage points a year faster than bond funds while avoiding the unnerving volatility of racier stock funds.

Total return funds that go 40% or more into fixed-income securities are about a third less volatile than those that traditionally keep 85% or more of their portfolios in stocks. Such stock-heavy total return funds are about 25% less topsy-turvy than pure growth funds. A total return fund's subcategory can give a quick insight as to where it fits on the continuum of stocks vs. bonds. Flexible-income funds, for example, rely most heavily on bonds, typically holding just 20% of their assets in stocks. Convertible securities funds store at least 60% of their money in bonds or dividend-paying preferred stock that can be traded in for shares of common stock. The trade-off? Convertibles typically yield one to three percentage points less than straight corporate bonds while offering at least half the potential capital appreciation of the issuer's common stock. Balanced funds aim for a roughly 60-40 split between stocks and bonds, compared with about 75-25 for equity income portfolios. By comparison, so-called growth and income funds tend to be at least 80% invested in stocks.

If you're considering total return funds that keep more than 20% of their assets in bonds, call the fund and request figures on its bonds' average weighted maturity and credit quality. As explained later in this chapter, short-term and intermediate issues hold their value far better than long-term bonds with maturities of 10 years or more when interest rates rise. Credit quality is also a concern on securities rated below investment grade (BB or lower from Standard & Poor's or Baa or lower from Moody's). The greater the proportion of suspect IOUs, the more susceptible the fund is to losses when the economy slows and issuers struggle to pay interest.

◆ TAP THE OLD HOMESTEAD FOR INCOME

More and more older homeowners are turning to reverse mortgages to supplement their retirement income. Think of a reverse mortgage as a spigot that allows you to pour your home equity into your pocket. You receive the money in fixed monthly payments, in one lump sum or as a line of credit. When you die, the lender taps the proceeds from the sale of the house to recapture the money it advanced you, up to the value of your home.

Fannie Mae enters the field. Although reverse mortgages have been marketed since the early 1980s, they've recently become more popular and easier for homeowners to evaluate. Last year the loan clearinghouse Fannie Mae (the Federal National Mortgage Association) made available its reverse mortgages. They let homeowners tap up to $207,000 of their equity, far more than the $155,250 limit maintained by the U.S. Department of Housing and Urban Development. In addition, President Clinton and Congress have agreed to let people apply for HUD's reverse mortgages if they own two- to four-unit properties and live in one. A fairly new federal law also requires lenders to show the total annual average cost of their reverse mortgages in writing so that you can easily see which ones offer the best deals.

Factor in a variety of costs. The tab depends on factors including the amount you borrow, the length of the loan and the value of your home. Lenders also take your life expectancy into account when they calculate how much you'll get. The older you are, the better the deal is for you. For example, a HUD reverse mortgage on a $150,000 home might let a 65-year-old receive $549 a month. A 75-year-old in the same town could get $728. Obviously, these plans are not for everyone. So before signing up or suggesting one to your parents, you should follow these steps.

Bone up on how reversers work. These loans can be mighty complicated. "You're not likely to get the best deal if you're forced to make a decision under pressure," notes Bronwyn Belling, a reverse-mortgage specialist at the American Association of Retired Persons. For a detailed explanation of reverse mortgages, get *Your New Retirement Nest Egg* by Ken Scholen ($25; 800-247-6553).

Comparison shop. Notes author Scholen: "The difference in what you'd receive from two lenders could be as much as $30,000." If your place is worth more than $207,000, you'll probably get the best deal from private lenders. For the names of lenders making reverse mortgages in your area, download the AARP's list from the internet (http://www.aarp.org).

Talk it over with family and advisers. Parents should run the idea by their kids. Though you may assume they'll object to depleting the home equity, they may surprise you. At least half of the 100,000 calls AARP gets about reverse mortgages each year are from adults inquiring for their parents.

◆ EARNING DEPENDABLE DIVIDENDS

Income-minded investors love bond funds that yield regular, generous dividends. Such funds are particularly attractive to retirees and other people who depend on investment earnings for a large portion of their everyday living expenses. Many growth-oriented investors also own the funds to help diversify their holdings and lower the risk inherent in fairly aggressive stock portfolios. Bonds obligate the issuing company or government to pay interest, usually at regular intervals, and to repay the face value of the bond at maturity. A large number of these funds provide tax-exempt income by investing exclusively in municipal bonds issued by city and state governments.

Unlike a bank certificate of deposit, a bond fund's yield isn't guaranteed. Your total return depends not only on the dividends you get but also on the price you receive when you sell your fund shares. The value of bonds (and the funds that own them) appreciates when interest rates decline and falls when interest rates increase. Generally speaking, the higher a bond fund's yield, the greater the overall credit risk, maturity and volatility of the bonds the fund holds. There is no credit risk, or likelihood of a bond's issuer defaulting on its interest or principal payments, among funds that invest solely in bonds or mortgage-backed securities guaranteed by the federal government. Nor should there be any fears over the safety of funds whose bond holdings have the highest credit ratings from Standard & Poor's or Moody's, which grade companies and municipalities from AAA (tops) to D (in default). Financially solid issuers pay the least to borrow money, so you get lower yields. To grab higher income, however, some funds concentrate on lower quality issues, commonly called junk bonds, that are rated less than investment grade (B or below). While remarkably few junk bonds have defaulted over time, they are the ones investors dump first when business conditions sour or bond prices slump across the board, causing their prices to drop the most.

Decide how to place your bond bets. Long-term bonds (maturing in more than 10 years) almost always yield more than intermediate issues (five to 10 years) or short-term ones (five years or fewer) because their prices are the most sensitive to fluctuations in interest rates. If rates were to rise by just one percentage point, the price of recently issued 20-year Treasury bonds would fall about 9%. Three-year Treasury notes would drop only 2% to 3%. So if you think interest rates are going to rise substantially, you should only consider funds that limit their holdings to bonds of short or intermediate terms. If you expect rates to fall, you would definitely favor long-term bond funds. Each fund generally keeps its holdings' maturities within a range specified in the prospectus. To find out a fund's average maturity, you must call the fund.

U.S. Governments. These funds invest in bonds issued by the U.S. Treasury or federal government agencies. The safety from default is all but absolute, which makes government funds tops for conservative income seekers. The trade-off is lower yields. Vanguard Fixed-Income Long-Term U.S. Treasury, for example, recently paid slightly less than Vanguard Fixed-Income Long-Term Corporate, a corporate fund of roughly the same average maturity. Note that in Treasury-only bond funds, the lower yield is partly made up by the fact that the dividends usually escape state taxes. Also be aware that government backing does not protect you against interest rate risk. A Treasury portfolio will drop in price when interest rates rise.

Mortgage-backed securities. One species of government fund specializes in these issues, which represent shares in investment pools consisting of home mortgages. They're backed by federal agencies with such cute nicknames as Ginnie Mae (the Government National Mortgage Association) and Freddie Mac (the Federal Home Loan Mortgage Corporation). They offer yields 0.5 to 1.5 percentage points higher than those on Treasury funds. The higher yields are partly a trade-off for prepayment risk, one peculiar to mortgage-backed securities. When interest rates fall, homeowners rush to refinance their mortgages at lower rates. As the old pooled mortgages are paid off, funds holding the securities are, in effect, handed back parts of their principal, which they then must reinvest at lower prevailing yields. Thus mortgage funds get a far smaller boost than Treasuries from falling rates.

Corporates. Such bond funds allow you to invest in businesses ranging from America's most solid to its shakiest. Entries in our high-grade corporate category hold bonds carrying an average credit rating only a step below governments, making them an appealing alternative for investors who want to earn more than government funds pay but who don't want to get swamped by credit risk. At the other end of the credit spectrum are high-yield corporates, better known as junk bond funds. They focus on the bonds of debt-burdened behemoths and unproven start-ups. Unlike other bond funds, junkers are at their best in a strengthening economy because a healthy business climate reduces the risk of defaults. Indeed, during the recent economic recovery, junk bond funds have been one of the hottest fixed-income categories. Lately, however, the yield spread between Treasuries and junk funds has been at the low end of their range. So high-yield issues don't have as much room to recreate the glory days of recent years.

Multisector. Such funds typically own a cross section of government, high-yield and even foreign bonds. Mark Wright, a fixed-income analyst at Morningstar, recommends one, Janus Flexible Income, for its astute asset diversification, which includes high-yield bonds, mortgage-backed securities, foreign bonds and Treasuries.

Tax-exempt municipals. These funds buy bonds issued by cities, states and other local government entities. Also known as municipal bond funds, all of them produce dividends free of federal income tax. The dividends from so-called single-state muni funds, which invest entirely within the borders of one state, are exempt from state and local taxes as well for resident shareholders. Muni funds are most appealing to people in the 28% federal tax bracket and above. Analysts say that a growing appetite for tax-frees and a shrinking supply also bodes well for muni prices. One reason is that aging baby boomers will increasingly need to save on a tax-sheltered basis. But you still need to be cautious. Unless otherwise stated in the prospectus, most muni funds tend to hold longer-term securities than comparable corporate or government funds, making the muni funds more sensitive to interest-rate fluctuations. Also check the fund's annual report to make sure that it isn't trying to pump up yield by loading up on the offerings of frequently shaky muni issuers like industrial development agencies or hospitals. Analysts say that the slight increase in yield just isn't worth the considerably greater default risk.

Foreign bonds. Diversification is the main reason to invest a portion of your fixed-income portfolio overseas. As in stocks, international diversification in bonds can reduce risk and enhance long-term gains. That's because the U.S. and foreign bond markets rarely move in unison. When one is down, the other is often rising. Remember, however, that foreign bond funds face the same currency risks discussed earlier. When you invest in foreign securities of any kind you run the risk that a rising dollar will shrink their value. Most international bond funds try to minimize such risks by using hedging techniques in the foreign exchange markets. Hedging can be expensive, shaving your fund's profits by as much as 5%. And fund managers can guess wrong about shifts in exchange rates. Thus investors with long time frames generally are better off buying foreign bond funds with a policy of riding out currency swings, which experts say tend to equalize over periods of five to 10 years.

◆ PROFITING THROUGH LIFE'S PASSAGES

By diversifying among stocks, bonds or cash, you offset losses in one asset category with gains in another. While diversification can't guarantee that you'll never lose money, it can reduce your portfolio's risk and improve your odds of reaching your goals. To determine the most efficient mix of investments, experts look at the correlation between various asset classes. Correlation is the technical term for comparing how different assets perform relative to one another over varying market cycles. You want to build a portfolio of different types of assets that are not closely correlated to one another. That way, you won't get clobbered by all your investments dropping in value at roughly the same time.

What's more, a properly diversified portfolio lets you put some of your money in potentially high-paying assets that otherwise might be too risky. You perform this alchemy by combining them with investments to which the high fliers are only weakly correlated. For example, a portfolio entirely invested in the large-company stocks that make up the S&P 500 would have gained over 14% a year during the past two decades. But you could have earned 16% a year over the same time frame with a portfolio invested 65% in S&P 500 stocks, 20% in overseas stocks and 15% in small-company shares. In allocating assets, the pros rely not only on stocks' and bonds' past performance but also on estimates of their potential future returns. These predictions are based on forecasts of how market cycles will affect the performance of different asset classes. The model portfolios found in this chapter are based on projections that over the next 10 years or so large-company stocks will return an average of 10% annually, bonds will earn 5% a year and cash investments such as Treasury bills will return 4% annually.

As you grow older, start a family and move closer to retirement, your investment goals and taste for risk change. Your portfolio should change along with you. Younger people, for example, can afford to aim for high returns with aggressive stock funds because they have many years to recover from market slumps. But as you get closer to retirement, you need to shift to a more cautious allocation that will preserve your gains. There's a second, equally powerful argument in favor of asset allocation. Academic studies show that about 90% of investors' returns come from the right combination of assets, with the remainder derived from their skill in picking securities and from timely trading. To help you design your own allocation, MONEY devised a model fund portfolio for each of the four major stages in most people's working lives–starting out, raising a family, peak earning years and retirement living (our depictions of the portfolios begin opposite).

Going for it in your 20s to early 30s. You now have
about 30 years before early retirement. So you can afford to gun for growth by stashing at least 75% of your portfolio in stock funds. Go for as much as 100% if you feel comfortable riding out market swings. Those who tend to get queasy in roller-coaster markets might put as much as 25% of their money in bond funds, which pay interest that will help stabilize most portfolios. Based on past performance, this 75-25 lineup has the potential to return over 9% annually.

For beginners with small savings, a single fund that buys large-company stocks is a sound choice. Blue chips tend to offer solid capital appreciation with less volatility than smaller stocks. Nervous investors might want to opt for a balanced or asset-allocation fund instead. These all-in-one portfolios typically keep about 60% of their assets in stocks and the rest in risk-cushioning bonds and other fixed-income investments. Investors who have $10,000 or more ought to assemble a diversified portfolio of funds. Allocate about 30% of your assets to large-company stocks, 25% to small-company stocks and 20% to overseas stocks. Small stocks historically have outpaced their bigger brothers, though with greater volatility. Overseas stocks can spice up your portfolio because many foreign economies are likely to grow much faster than ours over the next decade. The risks you face are political instability and adverse swings in the value of the dollar.

For a smoother ride to those higher returns, you might include both value and growth-stock funds in your portfolio. Value managers

Single person, late twenties, with $10,000 saved

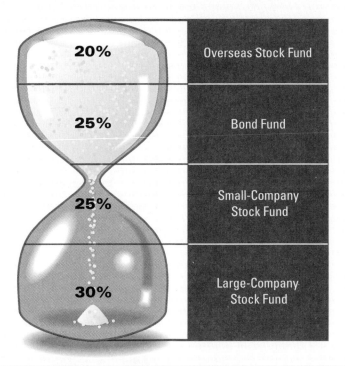

20%	Overseas Stock Fund
25%	Bond Fund
25%	Small-Company Stock Fund
30%	Large-Company Stock Fund

look for out-of-favor companies with share prices that do not fully reflect their earnings prospects or asset values. By contrast, growth-stock managers, as the name suggests, prefer companies with rapidly accelerating revenues and earnings, even though their shares typically will command premium prices. You can't really predict which investing style will be more successful in any given year. Studies show that over periods of 20 years or more, however, value has a slight performance advantage over growth.

As for your fixed-income holdings, put about 15% of your money in investment-grade bonds with intermediate maturities of five to 10 years. Studies show that five-year issues produce roughly 95% of the return of 30-year issues with only half the volatility. About 10% of your money should go into a convertible bond fund, which will give you a shot at capital gains, or to a high-yield fund, which takes on extra risk

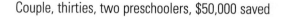

Couple, thirties, two preschoolers, $50,000 saved

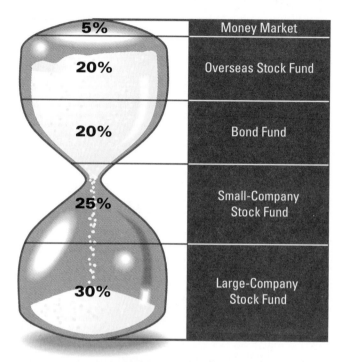

5%	Money Market
20%	Overseas Stock Fund
20%	Bond Fund
25%	Small-Company Stock Fund
30%	Large-Company Stock Fund

in pursuit of the fatter yields paid by junk bonds. But steer clear of bond funds that carry sales charges or fees that total more than 1% of net assets. Their managers generally can't overcome these high expenses with superior performance. (Fees are listed in a fund's prospectus.)

Family planning in your early 30s to 40s. With kids to provide for and mortgages to pay off, many investors in this age group reduce their portfolios' risk. Don't overdo it. You will be working another 20 years or more, so keep at least 75% of your money in stocks. You can achieve that balance by trimming your bond funds and moving the excess cash to a money-market fund. Our model is designed to give you average returns of about 8.5% annually. At this stage, you should further diversify your bond holdings. High earners should consider transferring the money in their convertible or high-yield corporate bond fund to a tax-free munic-

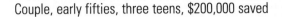

Couple, early fifties, three teens, $200,000 saved

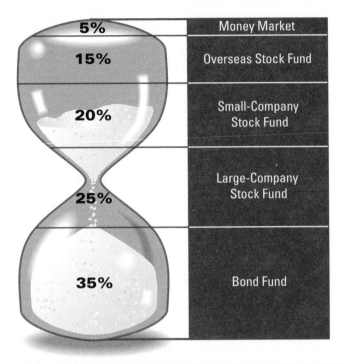

5%	Money Market
15%	Overseas Stock Fund
20%	Small-Company Stock Fund
25%	Large-Company Stock Fund
35%	Bond Fund

ipal bond fund and adding enough money so that it becomes 10% of the portfolio. A taxable alternative is an international bond fund. Fixed-income markets in the U.S. and abroad generally move in different directions. So you will offset a falling market with one that is on the rise. Foreign bond funds can respond sharply to currency fluctuations. But if you can let your money ride for at least 10 years, the swings will likely even out.

Cruising in your early 40s to 50s. You have reached your peak earning years–just in time to pay your kids' college bills. Don't let that serve as an excuse to neglect your savings. Stocks should still be the centerpiece of your portfolio. But ease back on risk by reducing your exposure to large-company stocks to 25%, small caps to about 20% and overseas stocks to 15%. This model aims to provide you with average total returns of around 8% annually. You can add greater sta-

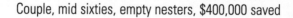

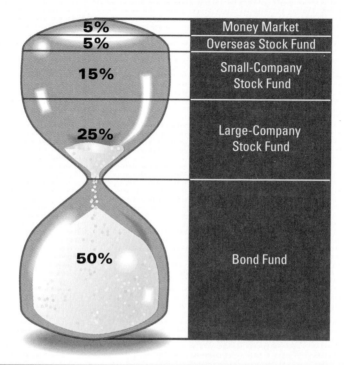

Couple, mid sixties, empty nesters, $400,000 saved

5%	Money Market
5%	Overseas Stock Fund
15%	Small-Company Stock Fund
25%	Large-Company Stock Fund
50%	Bond Fund

bility to your portfolio by emphasizing value funds. Since value funds focus on bargain-priced companies, they tend to fall less far than their high-flying growth peers during market corrections. And the stocks in value funds tend to pay dividends that will bolster your returns in down years. In the fixed-income portion of your portfolio, you might seek additional security by cutting international bonds to 5% and exchanging your intermediate-term corporate bond fund for one that holds government issues. Investors in the 28% bracket or above, however, will probably do better with tax-exempt bonds. To earn high returns with minimum risk, look for muni funds with annual fees of less than 1% that hold mainly bonds rated A or higher.

Throttling back in your early 50s to 60s. With retirement around the corner, you may be tempted to cash in your stock funds and tuck the proceeds into principal-preserving bond or money-market funds. That could prove to be a bad move. At 50 you still have a lifetime of at least 30 years ahead of you. If inflation stays at 3% a year, that will cut the purchasing power of today's dollar in half in only 12 years. Thus you should still hold a roughly 45% stake in stocks. Such a model portfolio should produce average returns of around 7.5% a year. In addition, now is an excellent time to move out of international bonds entirely and into U.S. Government issues for greater safety. Truly risk-averse investors might anchor their portfolios with Treasury notes, which come due in two to 10 years, because their principal at maturity and interest payments are federally guaranteed.

◆ MAKE YOUR MONEY LAST LONGER

How can you keep from running short of cash as you age? For starters, you must recognize that as you grow older, your retirement needs will change, just as they did during your working life. You'll be most active, and spend more on everything except healthcare, in your first decade of retirement before you turn 75 or so. Between 75 and 85, your out-lays could decline 20% or more as you stick closer to home and spend less on clothing, furniture and restaurant meals. By the third decade, your expenses might jump again as medical bills escalate. Meanwhile, your investment strategy must shift as your spending and tolerance for risk change.

Among the earliest decisions that most retirees encounter center around the right time to begin collecting Social Security and your company pension, if you have one. If you're now 58 or older, you can begin pocketing your monthly Social Security checks at age 62 and receive only 80% of the benefit you would get had you waited until you were 65. The age for full benefits is scheduled to rise gradually for people born after 1937 until it reaches 67 in 2027. But Congress may extend the minimum age for collecting your full benefits even further to help keep Social Security from going broke.

When to receive your checks. Apply for benefits at 62 if you're in poor health or need the money. Otherwise, wait until 65. Ask your local Social Security office to estimate your benefit, or call 800-772-1213 and ask for Form SSA-7004, the personal earnings and benefits estimate statement. You may want to delay taking Social Security until you're 70 if you're still working. That's because your benefits will be cut $1 for every $2 you earn above $8,280 between ages 62 and 65 and $1 for every $3 above $12,500 from 65 to 69. The threshold rises annually. Waiting until you're past 65 will also increase your payout. You'll get an extra 5% annually for each year that you put off receiving Social Security until you're 70.

You also need to ask your employee benefits office about your pension options. Taking your pension more than a couple of years before age 65 may cost you dearly. Many employers knock 6% off a pension for each year an employee retires before age 65. If that's true of your employer and you leave work at 64, your pension of, say, $1,000 a month will be trimmed to $940 for the rest of your life. Begin taking pension checks at 60, and you will wind up with $700 a month. In this case, keep working as long as you can, especially if you have few other financial resources.

Once you've figured out what you can count on from Uncle Sam and Mother Corp., turn your attention to your investments. Let's say you are 65 and your $200,000 in savings earns an average of 7% a year. Also assume that you start taking out about 8% annually, or $16,000, and boost the dollar amount of your withdrawals by 4% a year to offset inflation. Under this scenario, your pot will last 15 years. Of course, your cost of living in retirement may rise less than 4% a year. That would permit you to make smaller increases in your withdrawals, which will enable your money to last longer. The anecdotal evidence is that inflation for retirees is relatively low, maybe 1%. That's largely because retirees spend less on such price-sensitive items as autos, clothing and housing.

Easing into the early retirement years. You might initially plan to continue to work at least part time. That way, you can postpone tapping your savings and perhaps even add to them. By investing an extra $5,000 a year for five years, you could pay for two more years of retirement. Most retirees can't afford to leave their portfolios untouched, of course. So retirement experts suggest you reinvest all your interest and dividends and withdraw no more than 6% of your portfolio a year. You also could spend your interest and dividends and withdraw enough from your principal to make up the balance. Let's say you receive $3,000 in interest and dividends on your $100,000 portfolio. You could raise the other $3,000 by selling some of your holdings. Either approach should still allow you to leave generous sums to your heirs. To determine more precisely how much of your capital you can safely spend each year, either hire an accountant or run the numbers yourself on popular retirement planning software like *Quicken Financial Planner.*

When you begin spending some of your principal, make sure you consume the assets in taxable accounts first. This will allow the money in your 401(k), Keogh, IRA and other plans to continue compounding tax-free as long as possible. The payoff for following this strategy can be spectacular. Say you retire at 65 with $300,000 in your IRA and another $300,000 in taxable investment accounts, both earning 8% annually before taxes. If you withdrew $40,000 a year by tapping your IRA first, your money would run out by age 85. If you draw down the taxable account first, however, your tax-deferred savings would keep compounding. So you wouldn't run out of money until you're 97.

Unfortunately, you usually can't let tax-favored plans go untouched beyond age 70.5. Otherwise, the IRS will whack you with a stiff penalty amounting to 50% of what you should have taken out based on your life expectancy. (Under a new law, you're exempt from this rule if you are still working for the employer that sponsors your retirement plan and you don't own 5% or more of the company.) At 70.5, the IRS generally requires that you take out at least enough each year to exhaust your tax-deferred accounts over your expected life span.

Let's say you're nearly 71 and have $500,000 in your IRA. Your life expectancy would be 16 years. (For the IRS tables, call 800-829-3676 and ask for Publication 590.) That means you would have to pull out at least a sixteenth of your portfolio, or $31,250 annually. You can withdraw smaller amounts without penalty only by naming someone else as the joint beneficiary of your accounts. Then you can base your withdrawals on your joint life expectancy, which will be longer than if you relied on yours alone. For purposes of the calculation, however, unless the joint beneficiary is your spouse, the IRS limits the age difference between beneficiaries to 10 years. That means if you're 70 and name your infant grandchild as beneficiary, the kid is a mature 60 in the eyes of the IRS.

Settling into the middle retirement years. Check your portfolio at least every year to see whether your asset allocations need rebalancing. For instance, if a rambunctious bull market has boosted your stake in stocks or stock funds from 60% to 75%, you may be exposed to more risk than you want to be. Moreover, you have less time to make up for investment losses as you age. But don't cut back too much on stocks. Today's typical 77-year-old can expect to live 11 years. So hold around 40% of your portfolio in stocks to keep it growing so that you never run out of money even if you live beyond 100.

In finding the right allocation for you, take into account your personal circumstances. If you need to spend more cash, perhaps to pay medical costs, shift extra money into the short-term fixed-income portion of your portfolio. That will reduce the chance that you'll have to sell stocks at a loss to pay those bills. On the other hand, if you plan to leave an estate and you can comfortably handle investment risk, you may want to keep your stock holdings at their current level or even boost them slightly.

Enjoying the late retirement years. When your horizon is five or 10 years, you don't have much time to recover from market downturns. You therefore may want to prune back your stock holdings. If you have ample resources and dream of leaving an estate, keep more of your money in stocks. Retired businessman Arch Galloway, 84, and his wife Audrey have a whopping 70% of their portfolio in high-quality growth stocks such as Mobil and H.J. Heinz, some of which Galloway has owned for 30 to 40 years. Thanks to generous investment income, the Sarasota couple does not need to tap principal to make ends meet. "If I were to sell my stocks now, I'd have a devil of a capital gains tax to pay," Galloway says.

He would rather leave all his securities to his two children and six grandchildren, who won't owe taxes on the gains during his lifetime because the securities' tax cost will be stepped up to their current value when he dies. After four decades of investing, Galloway isn't spooked by talk of a looming bear market either. "I don't like to see the markets go down, but I know that every down is followed by an even greater up," he says. "I'm very definitely a long-term growth investor." You probably should be too. But, like Arch Galloway, make sure that your retirement plan reflects your appetite for risk and your circumstances.

◆ DON'T LET DIVORCE SMASH YOUR PLANS

Even longstanding marriages can be torn apart when children move out, careers plateau, aged parents die or future options seem to dwindle. The number of divorces among people over age 55 is a third higher than was the case 20 years ago. If your marriage breaks up, your shattered emotions may eventually heal. But your nest egg might not after you and your ex split up assets that have accumulated over many years. Here's how your retirement stockpile can dwindle in divorce.

Dividing assets. This can depend on the state in which you and your spouse live. While all courts must follow federal law in dealing with company-sponsored retirement plans, states have their own laws on splitting assets in IRAs and Keoghs. Courts in community-property states (Arizona, California, Idaho, Louisiana, Nevada, New Mexico, Texas, Washington and Wisconsin) usually require divorcing spouses to share assets in those plans equally. Other states give judges more discretion, often to the detriment of lower-paid spouses. Judges in these states generally award as much as two-thirds of the marital property that's contested to the higher wage earner. Whatever your share, it probably won't be enough to finance the retirement you've been planning.

Defined contribution. These plans may be 401(k)s, 403(b)s or SEPs (Simplified Employee Pensions) if you're salaried, or Keoghs and SEPs if you're self-employed. You may also have an IRA. If your plans and your spouse's are roughly equal in value, the court will likely let you both keep your plans intact. Otherwise, the judge may divide the total between you, instructing your employers in a court order which share belongs to each of you. Such plans are relatively easy to split up because they consist of company stock or money invested in securities. If the court divides your 401(k) in half, most companies will set up a separate account for your spouse's share. Henceforth, your contributions will go entirely into your account. Some companies will let ex-spouses withdraw everything in their accounts as lump sums that they can roll over into IRAs or take as cash. Other companies allow withdrawals over time, as with any retirement account. Either way, the law imposes no 10% penalty on withdrawals by ex-spouses who are younger than 59.5.

Defined benefit. To make things simple, many divorcing couples agree to let one spouse keep the traditional pension, while the other takes all or a portion of the 401(k)s and other defined-contribution accounts. If you must split a pension with your ex, most companies prefer you to use the so-called fixed date method. Here's how it generally works. Based on your salary and years of service, your benefits office will calculate what your pension would be if you were to retire on the day you expect your divorce to be final. Say you would qualify for a $10,000 pension on that date. A court might order your company to give your spouse $5,000 a year of your pension no matter how big your benefit actually turns out to be when you really retire. Your spouse would start to collect the $5,000 when he or she reaches retirement age (usually 65, though some companies permit earlier retirement). This could occur even if you're still working and not receiving your share of the pension.

Some companies let you use a more complicated calculation called the fractional method. Here's how it works. Divide the number of months you were married and employed at your company by the total number of months you've worked for your company, married or not. Next, multiply the result by your estimated pension benefit on the date you plan to retire. Finally, multiply that amount by the percentage of your pension the court has awarded to your spouse. Let's say you've been married 10 years, have worked at your company for 15 years and expect a $20,000 pension when you retire at age 65. Divide 120 by 180 and multiply the result (0.666) by $20,000, resulting in $13,320. If the court gives your spouse half your benefit, he or she would get $6,660 a year. You both take a gamble with this method, however, because you might opt to work beyond 65, thereby boosting your pension and your ex's share of it. If you take early retirement, your pension and your ex's share would be smaller. Whichever method you use, your ex can file for a cut of your pension at the earliest retirement age your company allows. But doing so freezes the amount your ex receives even if you continue to work and your benefits keep growing.

Social Security. An ex may collect up to 50% of the benefit a former spouse has earned when the ex begins receiving Social Security checks. When an ex files for benefits, Social Security automatically compares benefits from his or her own work record with benefits due as an ex-spouse and gives him or her the better deal. To determine whether you qualify for Social Security benefits as an ex-spouse, you must meet all four of these requirements: 1) your broken marriage must have lasted at least 10 years; 2) you must be 62 or older; 3) your ex must be at least 62 even if he or she isn't retired; 4) you must not be married to a new spouse.

4

MANAGE
YOUR MONEY
LIKE A PRO

*C*onscientious saving and a long-running bull market have helped many Americans amass a retirement portfolio that handily exceeds six figures. This nest egg often is supplemented by a small inheritance, a wad of company stock options or a hefty rollover from a 401(k) plan. While that kind of money won't necessarily change your life today, it should alter the way you invest. When you control a sizable portfolio, you typically will have a lot of assets to track. We offer help in this chapter with our worksheet, "Totting Up Your Assets and Liabilities," and evaluation of investment information that's now available on the internet in "Enhance Your Profits Online."

Having a bigger portfolio doesn't make investing any easier. As a high-net-worth individual, you are a target for every sales pitch on Wall Street. The truth is that money management is not rocket science. But it does require intelligent decision making to develop a coherent plan, diversify your investments, hire competent advisers and track your performance. The first mistake that affluent investors often make is failing to pick their advisers in any systematic way. You may let your personal banker steer some of your money to the trust department, where your stake is likely to be managed as part of a pooled fund. That's banking's version of a mutual fund. Then you might meet a stockbroker socially, be impressed and allot some dough to his or her firm's wrap account, where the brokerage firm parcels out your money among a team of prescreened money managers. As a result, you often have money in two or three places with no one making overall decisions or tracking how well the investments are performing.

To bring order to this expensive chaos, think about consolidating your money under just one or two umbrellas. If you invest primarily via funds, one of the most elegant solutions is to transfer all your far-flung accounts into a single one at a discount brokerage with a network of no-fee funds, as described later in "Today's Top Financial Supermarkets." Among them are Charles Schwab's One Source and Fidelity's Funds Network, both of which let you choose among hundreds of funds from dozens of fund families. Thus you can pick the best, not just those sponsored by one organization. And you can shift money around with no cost other than your share of the funds' annual expenses.

Anyone you hire to check over your portfolio should recommend a blend of assets that maximizes your return and shrinks your risk. By combining investments that rise and fall in different cycles, your whole portfolio will offer a better trade-off of risk and reward than any one of its parts. With a large portfolio, you can hire a broker or money manager to implement the blend for you on a discretionary basis–that is, without clearing each move with you. Money managers who invest directly in stocks often require minimum investments of $1 million or more. For topnotch firms with minimums of $10,000 or less, see "Hire Your Own Money Manager" in Chapter 5. Whomever you hire, you should insist on frequent updates about how your retirement portfolio is positioned. Having worked so hard to build a six-figure account, you no longer have to exert yourself quite as much to manage it. Let your advisers make your investments work as hard as they can. And let your money, not you, put in a few weekends for a change.

◆ HOW TO PICK WINNING STOCKS

As explained in the previous chapter, anyone old enough to oversee a sizable retirement portfolio probably knows that successful stockpicking strategies tend to be variations on the themes of value or growth. Value investors are those bargain shoppers who snap up stocks selling at a discount to what they believe is the stocks' real worth. Growth investors favor companies with superior earnings growth that they expect will propel the stock price upward. While those by-the-book definitions might be good enough to distinguish between types of stock funds, they are not much use in picking stocks that can beat the market. How do you know a stock's *real* worth, for example? For answers to this and other questions, we will walk you through the key attributes of top-performing value and growth stocks.

Neither style necessarily gives you a performance advantage over the short run. Studies show that, over 20 years or more, value stocks as a group have a two or three percentage point edge in annual return. In the real world, however, that edge is far from guaranteed. For the past 10 years, for example, the Russell 1000 growth index has returned 385% overall, slightly beating the 371% earned by the Russell 1000 value index. That's why you should own both types of stocks, depending on your particular risk tolerance and investing style.

Value investing requires the courage to buy unloved stocks, as well as the patience to hang on to them for three years or more until the market recognizes their value. "Value players have got to keep their emotions in check because they invest against the grain," says David Schafer, manager of Strong Schafer Value fund. Growth investing, on the other hand, appeals to quick-change artists. "You need to be optimistic but willing to move fast if things don't work out," says Sig Segalas, manager of Harbor Capital Appreciation. The risk is that your companies won't deliver on their anticipated earnings. Shareholders of growth firms often pay quickly and dearly for any earnings disappointment. So you should accept the risk that your stock could tumble 20% or more on bad news.

All the financial data discussed below can be found in references such as the *Value Line Investment Survey*, which is available in most public libraries. If you are wired into the internet, you can find similar information at investing sites such as http://www.wsrn.com.

Traits of growth stocks destined to rise. The easiest part of investing in growth stocks is finding companies that are expanding their earnings a brisk 15% to 20% a year. The toughest part is finding those that can continue their profit streak into the future. A growth stock ideally should clear all five hurdles below.

◆ **Annual profit growth of 15% or more.** Your starting point is the company's past performance. A five-year record of 15% earnings gains would put the company in the top 25% of the S&P 500 stocks and show you that growth is no fluke. Companies with these sterling records typically have dominant market share in an expanding industry like technology, healthcare or consumer products. A prime example of the latter is **Gillette** (traded on the NYSE, around $94), says analyst William Steele at Dean Witter in San Francisco. This $10 billion consumer-products behemoth racked up seven straight years of double-digit earnings growth from worldwide sales of its razors, toiletries and other products. The company acquired Duracell's battery line in late 1996, which may lift earnings slightly this year. Says Steele: "Once Gillette digests the acquisition, it is likely to keep growing at a 16% rate, or twice as fast as the market, over the next three years." He also thinks the stock can appreciate at least 15% over the next 12 months.

◆ **Projected earnings growth of 15% or more.** With most forecasters looking for the S&P 500's profit growth to slow to just 7% or 8% over the next year, reliable large-cap growth stocks should be expected to deliver 15% or better profit increases next year and average the same amount over the following two. Earnings predictions are subject to frequent revision, however, making them the shakiest pillar supporting the case for any growth stock. To minimize this uncertainty, stick with companies where the business plan that's expected to drive future growth is already securely in place. One example is $38 billion **Hewlett-Packard**, the Palo Alto-based computermaker (NYSE, around $55). The growth of the company has slowed from a blistering 30% rate to a more sustainable 15% recently. But Segalas expects that its perennially best-selling inkjet printers and supplies, plus a successful new line of digital photo equipment, will help keep that 15% secure for at least three years. Segalas is looking for the stock to return at least 15% over the next 12 months.

◆ **Annual sales growth of 10% or better.** If the bottom line is growing but sales are not, it may be an indication that earnings growth is coming entirely from cost cutting. Conversely, booming revenues and decreasing profits say the company is losing control of its outlays. Both mean that earnings will eventually stop growing. An ideal pick will show five-year growth on both the top and bottom lines. Take, for example, $2.2 billion **Amgen** (over the counter, around $59). The Thousand Oaks, Calif. biotech firm has notched sales gains at a heady 30% annual rate for the past five years, while its earnings have climbed an average of 20% a year. Brian Spengemann, head of Coventry Capital, a Chicago money-management firm, expects sales of Amgen's leading blood cell therapies, Neupogen and Epogen, to continue increasing around 20% annually for the next three years as the applications of these therapies expand. That should result in healthy earnings growth of 17%, which Spengemann says should lift the stock about 30% over the next 12 to 18 months.

Here's how to figure out what you (and your spouse) have now amassed in household net worth. In valuing company pensions, call your (and your spouse's) benefits department.

ASSETS	VALUE
Cash/equivalents	
Cash on hand, checking account(s)	$ _____
Money-market account(s)	_____
Certificates of deposit	_____
Securities	
Stocks	_____
Bonds	_____
Mutual funds	_____
Limited partnerships	_____
Retirement plans	
IRAs	_____
401(k)s	_____
Profit sharing	_____
Pension	_____
Insurance	
Cash-value life	_____
Annuities	_____
Real estate	
Primary residence	_____
Vacation property	_____
Rental property	_____
Land	_____
Antiques/collectibles	_____
Business equity	_____
Personal property/autos/other	_____
TOTAL	_____

DEBTS	BALANCE
Real estate loans	
Primary home mortgage	$ _____
Second mortgage/home-equity loan	_____
Home-equity line of credit	_____
Vacation home mortgage	_____
Investment property loan	_____
Installment loans	
Auto	_____
Education	_____
Credit-card balances	_____
Brokerage account loans	_____
Insurance policy loan	_____
401(k) loans	_____
Other	_____
TOTAL	_____

ASSET TOTAL	_____
DEBT TOTAL	_____
NET WORTH	_____

◆ **Return on equity of 20% or more.** Return on equity (ROE), which is net income divided by shareholders' equity, measures the company's overall profitability. Higher is better as long as the company hasn't leveraged its profits too much by taking on debt. In general, debt should not exceed 50% of shareholders' equity. Dave Fowler, co-manager of Vanguard U.S. Growth, looks for low-debt stocks whose ROE ranks in the top third of the S&P 500, which means 20% or better. One such paragon is $32 billion **Pepsico** (NYSE, around $37) with a rich ROE of 23. The Purchase, N.Y. company plans to spin off its low-profit restaurants. Fowler believes that, freed of these shackles, Pepsico management should be able to expand earnings at a 15% rate. "Assuming no major change in market conditions," he says, "Pepsico's stock price is likely to appreciate about 17% over the next 12 to 18 months."

◆ **Earnings multiple in line with growth.** Sometimes investors' expectations can be so high that even the sturdiest growth machine is bound to disappoint—with ugly consequences for shareholders. You can reduce that risk by comparing your stock's PE (price-earnings multiple), based on its estimated next 12 months' profits, with its projected three-year annual profit growth. If the PE is more than 25% higher than the growth rate, the stock may be too expensive. You ideally would like to find a fast-growing company trading at a PE that's less than its growth rate. That's why Standard & Poor's Robert Natale has his eye on **3Com** (over the counter, around $48). This Santa Clara, Calif. networking company recently agreed to acquire modem manufacturer U.S. Robotics. 3Com was trading at a PE of 15 partly because of a temporary earnings shortfall. But Natale estimates that 3Com's long-term growth rate will be on the order of 30% to 40% annually thanks to continued strong demand for networking products. If he's right, he can see the stock rising more than 40% over the next 12 months.

Traits of value stocks headed higher. Value investors

tend to reject the growth buyer's obsession with predicting the future. They prefer to uncover undervalued assets in a company's here and now even if it's not entirely clear how and when the market will realize that value. As Warren Buffett, the nation's most famous value investor, summed up his philosophy: "If I can buy a dollar for 50¢, something good might happen to me." The problem is that undervalued assets tend to reside only in companies that have run into difficulty or that are part of unpopular industries like steel and forest products. To protect yourself, you should look for these value-revealing attributes:

◆ **Earnings multiple well below its peers.** "If a stock is selling at a significant PE discount to others in its industry, then it's worth a close look," says fund manager David Schafer. That's certainly true for $1.5 billion **Borg–Warner Automotive** (NYSE, around $50). This Chicago firm manufactures transmissions for cars and trucks and recently grinded along at 10 times earnings. That's among the lowest PEs in its industry in part because of its short track record since it was spun off from Borg-Warner in 1993. Says Schafer: "This company is the Rodney Dangerfield of the auto parts business–it can't get respect." But he thinks earnings at Borg-Warner Automotive have the potential to rebound 25% this year as more auto companies outsource their parts manufacturing. Then he expects growth to settle down to a still respectable 10% rate in 1998. As the company finally gets Wall Street's respect, the stock's PE figures to rise 40% to 14 and its price could climb 35% over the next 12 months.

◆ **Share price below 2.5 times book value.** A company's book value equals its assets minus its liabilities. So if the stock trades at less than its per-share book value, you can essentially buy the company for less than the value of the things it owns. With the S&P's current price-to-book value at 3.8, a ratio of less than 2.5 is a tough hurdle to clear. But William Browne, co-manager of the Tweedy Browne Global Value fund, has identified some gems in real estate stocks. His favorite is **Hovnanian Enterprises** (American Stock Exchange, around $6), a $808 million home builder based in Red Bank, N.J. "The stock is trading at $7 a share," notes Browne, "while its book value is $8.33, or 19% more." Weak sales on the East Coast have penalized earnings, but revenues are improving as home sales strengthen there. In addition, the company has a $291 million backlog of construction projects. Browne, who typically holds stocks for three years, thinks the stock could rise close to 50% over that period.

◆ **Long–term debt less than 50% of equity.** Investors don't buy value stocks, they marry them. So make sure that debt won't destroy your relationship. Value buyers, like many growth investors, usually say that you have an adequate margin of safety if long-term debt is less than 50% of shareholders' equity. The lower the percentage, the less risk.

One company that easily meets this standard, according to Eric Ryback, manager of the Lindner Dividend fund, is **Novell** (over the counter, around $7). This $1.4 billion networking company has absolutely no long-term debt. Soft foreign sales and increased domestic competition from Microsoft's Windows NT have pummeled the stock. But Ryback expects the Orem, Utah firm's new CEO, Eric Schmidt, to speed up a turnaround by expanding marketing efforts. And Novell is potential takeover bait for a networking software maker seeking to expand. "Any acquirer is likely to pay much more than $7 a share," predicts Ryback.

◆ **Consistent five–year profit growth.** To minimize their risk still further, bargain-hunting value investors also want steady or expanding profits. Schafer, for one, prefers companies whose earnings growth figures to outpace that of the S&P 500. One such inexpensive paragon is $5.5 billion **New Holland** (NYSE, around $27.). Spun off last year from Fiat, this Dutch company now ranks as the world's second largest agricultural equipment maker. "New Holland hasn't gotten the attention it deserves," says Schafer. He notes that some 30% of the company's sales are in fast-growing emerging markets, where improving living standards call for a more varied diet and thus better farming methods. In the next three years, he thinks emerging market appetites will help propel profit growth 10% or more annually. And Schafer looks for the stock to appreciate about 35% over the next 12 to 18 months.

◆ WAYS YOU CAN HEDGE YOUR BETS

Professional investors who share MONEY's cautious market outlook can easily hedge, or offset the risk of, stock portfolios with stock-index futures and other, more arcane instruments commonly called derivatives. Most individual investors, however, tend to shun such strategies as too complicated, risky and expensive. But look again. Below we explain three hedging maneuvers that, if used intelligently, can sharply reduce your risk.

A short course on put and call options. An option is a contract that allows you to buy or sell stock at a specified price until a certain date. The key point to note is that an option gives you the right to buy or sell but doesn't require you to do so. Let's say that you want to protect the profits you've earned on 100 shares of XYZ Corp., which trades for $60 a share. Buying a put option that can be exercised at $60 gives you the right to sell your stock for that price, which is known as the strike price. Even if your stock drops to $50, you still have a guaranteed right to sell it for $60 to the person who sold the $60 put option. That means you've locked in your full profit no matter what happens in the market.

Why would someone sell such an option and take the risk of having to buy a stock for more than the market price? Because the people who sell put options are betting that the money they earn by selling the options will add up to more than any losses they get stuck with. Moreover, put options sell at high premiums. An option that runs for a year can cost as much as 10% of the underlying stock's value. By contrast, the annual cost of homeowners insurance typically runs half a percent of the home's value. Still, buying insurance on your stock can be worth the stiff price if you sense that share prices are about to dive.

There's another type of stock option known as a call, which is the opposite of a put. A call option gives the buyer the right to purchase a particular stock at a specified price within a certain time period. Here are three smart ways small investors can use options to limit their risk and keep costs reasonably low.

Buy put options with reduced strike prices. As explained above, you could protect XYZ for about seven months at $60 by buying a put with a $60 strike price. But that would be expensive at about $400 for 100 shares. So, as with any form of insurance, your best bet is to reduce your premium by increasing your deductible. You could buy a $55 put, cutting your cost for 100 shares to about $200. Of course, a $55 put provides protection only if your stock drops below $55. The first $5 per-share loss (or $500 in our example) would come out of your pocket.

Sell call options against stock you own. If you sell a call option on a stock in your portfolio, known to the pros as writing a covered call, you effectively lower your purchase price on the stock by the amount you receive for the option. That will reduce the price at which you break even on your investment. Let's say you paid $50 a share for those 100 shares of XYZ. If you write a 13-month $60 call option on your shares for $713, you've effectively lowered your outlay for the stock from $5,000 to $4,287. Therefore, if the stock price drops back to $50, you'll still earn $713 instead of seeing all your profit wiped out.

Writing calls has two catches, however. First, if your stock rises in price, you'll either have to sell it at the option price or buy back your call. This can be expensive. If the 100 XYZ shares that you originally bought for $50 a share rise from $60 to $70 and you've sold a $60 call, you could be forced to sell your holding for $6,000. All together, you would have a total profit of $1,713 (including the $713 option premium) instead of the $2,000 you would have earned if you had never sold the option. Or you could buy back your call for around $1,000 and hope that the stock price keeps climbing, so that you come out ahead. To avoid this problem, never sell an option on any stock you aren't willing to give up. The second problem with selling calls is that the strategy doesn't offer much protection against really big stock declines. You can lower your break-even point on 100 shares of XYZ to $4,287 by writing a $60 call for $713. But that's little solace if the stock, which cost you $50 a share, falls to $30. Because of these two limitations, covered calls are best for stable stocks with limited risk.

Create an option collar as a cushion. Buying puts and selling calls on the same stock is known as a collar, probably the most cost-effective protection against a market downturn. You use the premium earned from selling the call to help pay the premium on the put. Suppose you owned 100 shares of ABC when the price was $97. If you sold a $120 call set to expire in January 1998, you would earn a $525 premium. You could use that money to help pay for a January 1998 put with a $90 strike price, which would have cost $625, or only $100 more than what you earned on the call. (For simplicity, we've left out commissions, which would run a total of about $80.) If ABC's price were to go down anytime this year, you wouldn't lose more than $7 a share. By contrast, you could earn as much as $23 a share if the stock rises to $120 or higher. No casino in the world will give you odds like that.

◆ CHECK OUT THESE NO-LOAD STOCKS

You can now bypass brokers and their commissions simply by purchasing shares directly from more than 100 U.S. and foreign companies. For a listing of firms that sell shares directly to the general public, see the table "Stocks You Can Buy From the Source" beginning on the next page. New companies are launching direct-purchase plans almost every

| COMPANY/SYMBOL | MINIMUM INVESTMENTS | TRANSACTION FEES[1] | | ANNUAL FEE | PHONE SALES | AUTOMATIC PLAN | TELEPHONE (800) |
		TO BUY	TO SELL				
ABT Building Products (ABTC)	$250/$50	$5/8¢	$10/8¢	None	N	Y	774-4117
Advanta (ADVNB)	1,500/50	None	$15/12¢	None	N	N	225-5923
Aegon (AEG)	250/50	$5/12¢	$5/12¢	$15	Y	Y	749-1687
Aflac (AFL)	750/50	None	None/5¢	None	N	Y	227-4756
Air Touch (ATI)	500/100	$7.50/10¢	$7.50/10¢	None	N	N	233-5601
American Rec. Centers (AMRC)	100/25	None	$2.50/None	None	N	N	522-6645
Ameritech (AIT)	1,000/100	$5/10¢	$10/12¢	$15/10¢[3]	Y	Y	233-1342
Amoco (AN)	450/50	Up to $3/7¢	$10/12¢	$8.50[3]	Y	Y	821-8100
Amway Japan (AJL)	250/50	$5/12¢	$5/12¢	$15	Y	Y	749-1687
Arrow Financial (AROW)	300/50	None	None	None	N	N	278-4353
Atlantic Energy (ATE)	250/0	None/5¢	None/18¢	None	N	Y	645-4506[4]
Atmos Energy (ATO)	200/25	None	$5/None	None	N	Y	382-8667
Augat (AUG)	250/100	None	$10/15¢	$5[3]	N	Y	575-3400[5]
Banco Santander (STD)	250/50	$5/12¢	$5/12¢	$15	Y	Y	749-1687
Bard (BCR)	250/25	Up to $10/3¢	$15/12¢	$15/3¢[3]	Y	Y	828-1639
Barnett Banks (BBI)	250/25	None	None/10¢	None	N	Y	328-5822
Bob Evans Farms (BOBE)	50/10	None	None	None	N	Y	272-7675
BRE Properties (BRE)	500/100	None	$15/12¢	None	N	Y	368-8392
British Airways (BAB)	250/50	$5/12¢	$5/12¢	$15	Y	Y	749-1687
British Telecom (BTY)	250/50	$5/12¢	$5/12¢	$15	Y	Y	749-1687
Cadbury Schweppes (CSG)	250/50	$5/12¢	$5/12¢	$15	Y	Y	749-1687
Capstead Mortgage (CMO)	250/50	None	$5/10¢-25¢	None	N	Y	527-7844
Carpenter Technology (CRS)	500/25	$10/10¢	$10/12¢	$10/10¢[3]	Y	Y	822-9828
Central & South West (CSR)	250/25	None	None/4¢	None	N	Y	527-5797
CMS Energy (CMS)	500/25	None	None/10¢	None	N	Y	286-9182
Comsat (CQ)	250/50	None	$5/6¢	None	N	N	524-4458
Conrail (CRR)	250/50	Up to $10/ 3¢	$15/12¢	$15[3]	Y	Y	243-7812
Crown American (CWN)	100/100	None	None/$25-30¢	None	N	N	278-4353
Dassault (DASTY)	250/50	$5/12¢	$5/12¢	$15	Y	Y	749-1687
Dominion Resources (D)	250/40	None	None/2.5¢	None	N	Y	552-4034
DQE (DQE)	100/10	None/5¢	None/7¢	$5[3]	N	Y	247-0400
DTE Energy (DTE)	100/25	$1/4¢	None/$12	None	N	N	551-5009
Duke Realty (DRE)	250/100	None	None/5¢-10¢	None	N	Y	278-4353

Notes: [1]Transaction fees are expressed as a flat fee plus a cost per share and are subject to change. Some companies may charge a small additional fee if they buy shares on the open market. [2]Shares must be sold through a broker. [3]One-time setup fee per share applies. Area codes: [4]609, [5]617, [6]888, [7]808, [8]201. **Sources:** Charles Carlson, the companies.

COMPANY/SYMBOL	MINIMUM INVESTMENTS	TRANSACTION FEES[1] TO BUY	TRANSACTION FEES[1] TO SELL	ANNUAL FEE	PHONE SALES	AUTOMATIC PLAN	TELEPHONE (800)
Eastern Co. (EML)	$250/$50	None	Up to $10/None	$5[3]	N	Y	774-4117
Empresa (ELE)	250/50	$5/12¢	$5/12¢	$15	Y	Y	749-1687
Energen (EGN)	250/25	None	$10/8¢	None	N	Y	774-4117
Enron (ENE)	250/25	None	$15/12¢	$17[3]	Y	Y	519-3111
Entergy (ETR)	1,000/100	$5/None	$15/12¢	None	N	N	225-1721
Equitable Cos. (EQ)	500/50	None	$10/12¢	None	N	Y	437-8736
Exxon (XON)	250/50	None	$5/10¢	None	N	Y	252-1800
Fiat (FIA)	250/50	$5/12¢	$5/12¢	$15	Y	Y	749-1687
First Commercial (FCLR)	500/25	None	N.A.[2]	None	N	N	482-8430
General Growth (GGP)	200/50	$5/5¢	$10/15¢	$15[3]	Y	Y	291-3713[6]
Grand Metropolitan (GRM)	250/50	$5/12¢	$5/ 12¢	$15	Y	Y	749-1687
Guidant (GDT)	250/50	Up to $7.50/3¢	$15/12¢	$15/3¢[3]	Y	Y	537-1677
Hawaiian Electric (HE)	100/25	None	$10/7¢	None	N	Y	532-5841[7]
Hillenbrand (HB)	250/100	$5/10¢	$10/10¢	None	N	Y	445-4802
Home Depot (HD)	250/25	Up to $2.50/5¢	$5/15¢	$5[3]	N	Y	730-4001
Home Properties (HME)	2,000/50	None	None/30¢	None	N	N	278-4353
Houston Industries (HOU)	250/50	None/5¢-10¢	None/5¢-10¢	None	N	N	231-6406
Illinova (ILN)	250/25	None	None/5¢	None	N	Y	750-7011
Imperial Chemical (ICI)	250/50	$5/12¢	$5/12¢	$15	Y	Y	774-4117
Integon (IN)	500/50	None	$10/12¢	7.50[3]	Y	Y	446-2617
Interchange Financial (ISB)	100/25	None/20¢-45¢	N.A.[2]	None	N	N	703-2265[8]
Ipalco Enterprises (IPL)	250/25	None/6¢	None/6¢	None	N	Y	847-2526[6]
Johnson Controls (JCI)	50/50	None	None/3¢-5¢	None	N	N	828-1489
Kellwood (KWD)	100/25	None	None	None	N	N	321-1355
Kerr-McGee (KMG)	750/10	None	None	None	N	N	786-2556
Madison G&E (MDSN)	50/25	None/8¢	None/8¢	None	N	N	356-6423
McDonald's (MCD)	1,000/100	$5/10¢	$10/10¢	$3/$5[3]	Y	Y	228-9623
Mid American Energy (MEC)	250/25	None/5¢	None/5¢	None	N	N	247-5211
Minnesota P&L (MPL)	250/10	None	$5/None	None	N	N	535-3056
Mobil (MOB)	250/10	None	$5/10¢	None	N	N	648-9291
Morton International (MII)	1,000/50	Up to $10/12¢	$15/12¢	$10[3]	Y	Y	990-1010
National Westminster (NW)	250/50	$5/12¢	$5/12¢	$15	Y	Y	749-1687
Nippon Telegraph & Tel. (NTT)	250/50	$5/12¢	$5/12¢	$15	Y	Y	749-1687
Norsk Hydro (NHY)	250/50	$5/12¢	$5/12¢	$15	Y	Y	749-1687
Novo-Nordisk (NVO)	250/50	$5/12¢	$5/12¢	$15	Y	Y	749-1687

◆ Stocks You Can Buy From the Source

| COMPANY/SYMBOL | MINIMUM INVESTMENTS | TRANSACTION FEES[1] | | ANNUAL FEE | PHONE SALES | AUTOMATIC PLAN | TELEPHONE (800) |
		TO BUY	TO SELL				
Oklahoma G&E (OGE)	$250/$25	None	None	None	N	Y	395-2662
Oneok (OKE)	100/25	None	None	None	N	Y	395-2662
Pacific Dunlop (PDLPY)	250/50	$5/12¢	$5/12¢	$15	Y	Y	749-1687
Peoples Energy (PGL)	250/25	None	None/8¢	None	N	Y	901-8878
Pharmacia & Upjohn (PNU)	250/50	$3/8¢	$10/8¢	None	N	Y	323-1849
Philadelphia Suburban (PSC)	500/25	None	None/6¢	None	N	N	205-8314
Piedmont Natural Gas (PNY)	250/25	None	None/9¢	None	N	Y	633-4236
Pinnacle West (PNW)	50/0	None/3¢	None/3¢	None	N	Y	457-2983
Procter & Gamble (PG)	250/100	$2.50/4¢	$2.50/4¢	$5[3]	N	Y	764-7483
Rank Group (RANKY)	250/50	$5/12¢	$5/12¢	$15	Y	Y	749-1687
Reader's Digest (RDA)	1,000/100	$5/12¢	$15/12¢	None	N	Y	230-2771
Regions Financial (RGBK)	500/25	None	$10/12¢	None	Y	Y	922-3468
Reuters (RTRSY)	250/50	$5/12¢	$5/12¢	$15	Y	Y	749-1687
Scana (SCG)	250/25	None	None/11¢-78¢	None	N	Y	763-5891
Sears Roebuck (S)	500/50	Up to $7.50/3¢	$15/12¢	$10/3¢[3]	Y	Y	732-7788[6]
Sony (SNE)	250/50	$5/12¢	$5/12¢	$15	Y	Y	749-1687
TDK (TDK)	250/50	$5/12¢	$5/12¢	$15	Y	Y	749-1687
Telmex (TMX)	250/50	$5/12¢	$5/12¢	$15	Y	Y	749-1687
Tenneco (TEN)	500/50	Up to $3/3¢	$10/12¢	None	Y	Y	446-2617
Texaco (TX)	250/50	None/5¢	None/5¢	None	N	Y	283-9785
Tyson Foods (TYSNA)	250/50	None	$10/12¢	$7.50[3]	Y	Y	822-7096
U S West Comm. (USW)	300/25	None	None/6¢	$4	Y	Y	537-0222
U S West Media (UMG)	300/25	$1/None	None/6¢	None	Y	Y	537-0222
Unilever (UN)	250/50	$5/12¢	$5/12¢	$15	Y	Y	749-1687
Urban Shopping Centers (URB)	500/50	Up to $3/10¢	$10/10¢	$7.50[3]	Y	Y	992-4566
Utilicorp United (UCU)	250/50	None	$20/12¢	None	Y	Y	884-5426
Viad (VVI)	100/10	None	None	None	Y	N	453-2235
Wal-Mart Stores (WMT)	250/50	$5/10¢	$20/10¢	$20/10¢[3]	Y	N	438-6278
Western Resources (WR)	250/20	None/Up to 5¢	None/7¢	None	N	Y	527-2495
Whitman (WH)	250/50	$5 /3¢	$15/12¢	$10/3¢[3]	Y	Y	446-2617
Wisconsin Energy (WEC)	50/25	None	None/5¢-10¢	None	Y	N	558-9663
WPS Resources (WPS)	100/25	None	None/20¢-25¢	None	N	N	236-1551
York International (YRK)	1,000/100	None	$15/12¢	None	N	Y	437-6726

Notes: [1]Transaction fees are expressed as a flat fee plus a cost per share and are subject to change. Some companies may charge a small additional fee if they buy shares on the open market. [2]Shares must be sold through a broker. [3]One-time setup fee per share applies. Area codes: [4]609, [5]617, [6]888, [7]808, [8]201. **Sources:** Charles Carlson, the companies.

week, spurred on by SEC rulings that encourage such programs. By the end of this year, an estimated 400 firms will be selling their stock directly to the public, predicts Charles Carlson, who wrote the book *No-Load Stocks* to promote the idea of buying stocks from the company.

Lower costs are the main appeal. Some companies charge nothing at all when you buy or sell. Most collect modest transaction fees of $5 to $10 plus 3¢ to 12¢ a share. Say you want to buy 100 shares of Cadbury Schweppes, recently trading at $34. The company will charge you $5 plus 12¢ a share, or a total of $17. Schweppes also charges an annual administrative fee of $15. In contrast, you would pay $36 to $50 at a typical discount broker and as much as $90 or so at a full-service firm.

When trading with the company, you can make small investments that just wouldn't be practical using a broker. Many companies require only $250 to $1,000 for your first purchase and as little as $50 after that. The company will give you fractional shares if your investment doesn't cover an even number of them. The minimum commission at a broker would consume more than half of such a tiny investment. Moreover, many companies now allow you to have money taken from your bank account at regular intervals to purchase additional shares. You can receive dividends in the form of additional stock. Some firms permit you to sell your shares by telephone; others require written instructions to sell. And about a dozen companies allow you to put your shares into an IRA.

What's in it for the company? Direct-purchase programs attract individual investors who otherwise might not buy the stock. They tend to be the buy-and-hold investors that corporate executives like because, unlike many professionals, they don't dump their shares at the first hint of bad news. And every new stockholder is a potential customer.

Our table gives vital statistics on companies that are selling their shares directly. The table tells you what the company charges when you buy and sell shares and whether it offers such features as automatic investing and telephone redemptions.

◆ EXPLOIT YOUR FIRM'S STOCK OPTIONS

Once reserved for CEOs and senior managers, stock options have become a popular way to motivate all employees by tying their interests to those of the shareholders. If you haven't been granted any options yet, chances are you will be. Even the servers who prepare your caffè latte at Starbucks Coffee get them if they work at least 20 hours a week. Among higher-ups, they're even more common. A survey of large manufacturing and service companies found that 73% offer options to middle managers. The typical package for someone making $80,000 to $100,000 has an expected future value ranging from 15% to 22% of base salary. Your stock options often come with a thick binder of rules about exercising them. Unfortunately, these instructions usually seem to be written by the same folks who produce manuals for VCRs. You're going to have to tackle yours sometime. But here's the short form to tide you over until then plus some suggestions on how to maximize what can be one of your most bountiful perks.

How your stock options work. Options give you the right, usually for a 10-year period, to purchase a specified number of shares of company stock at the fair market price the day the options were granted to you. This is known as the grant price. You are not obliged to buy stock; you can allow your options to expire unexercised. But this is usually not a smart thing to do. Mother Corp. has issued them to you so that you can make a small killing from any increase in the stock price brought about by your hard work. You can exercise your option (that is, buy the stock) for cash, swap company stock that you already own, or engage in what's known as a "cashless exercise." That's where you borrow from your stockbroker the money to exercise and then sell the stock, paying off the loan with part of the proceeds. Being generous but no patsy, Mother Corp. is likely to put two obstacles in your way. Nearly half the companies that offer options prohibit cashless exercises because they want to discourage quick sales. And most companies require you to become vested in your options over some period of time, usually one to five years, before you can exercise them.

Chances are, your options are the type known as nonqualified. The other kind are called incentive stock options (ISOs). The main difference between the two is how the IRS treats them. Nonqualified options require you to pay ordinary income tax on the difference between the grant price and the price of the stock on the day you exercise. If you hold the shares, you'll pay capital-gains tax on any additional gains in the stock when you sell. Companies prefer giving nonqualified options because the IRS treats them like wages, allowing the company to deduct the spread as an expense. ISOs are less popular because they give the company no tax advantage at all. But they offer you a big one. If you sell the shares one year or more after you exercise the option and more than two years after the option was granted, you pay no ordinary income tax at all, and only a capital-gains levy on the gain from the grant price to the sale price. That's why ISOs tend to be a perk for the top brass whose salaries put them in the highest tax brackets.

When to exercise your options. Faced with all these time limits and tax rules, every option holder needs a strategy. Your main worry is the timing. Early in the term of the options, you generally are advised to exercise if the stock price doubles. If that doesn't happen, wait until you draw within three years of the options' expiration date. That's a wide enough window of time for the stock to experience at least one healthy jump and give you your signal to exercise. Your next biggest worry is coming up with the money to exercise these things. The price tag can be considerable. Say you have a nonqualified grant of 500 shares at $30 and the stock price is at $50. If you paid cash, you'd have to ante up $15,000 for the shares plus $2,800 to cover the minimum 28% in withholding taxes. If you don't happen to have nearly $18,000 lying around, you have the alternatives of a cashless exercise or a stock swap, if your company allows them.

Factor in your tax bracket. If you have built up a thick file of stock options over your career, exercising all at once could catapult you into a higher tax bracket. For example, if you're married and file jointly with taxable income of $125,000, exercising $20,000 worth of nonqualified stock options would pop you from the 31% club to the 36% group. To avoid giving the IRS that kind of windfall, plan to exercise over a period of years.

Study your company's policy. Some firms require managers at your level to hold a multiple of their salary in company stock, typically about one times salary. As an incentive, some of these firms give you 10 shares for every 100 shares you retain. At those companies, you obviously have a reason to hang on to your shares after you exercise. But financial advisers frown on keeping more than 5% to 12% of your portfolio in the house stock. If your employer insists, of course, you don't have a choice. What if you quit your job? Your company will probably cancel your options, although some firms may give you as long as three months to exercise the vested ones. You might be able to get a new employer to make up for any option profits you forgo. But if you are thinking of leaving and the stock price has risen substantially, you should exercise now. If you retire, chances are your company will give you until the term is up to exercise unexpired options. If your income tax bracket will drop significantly after retirement, consider waiting to exercise until the year you plan to leave.

Don't rely on your memory. Many people make the mistake of stashing their option agreement in the safe-deposit box and forgetting about it. True, some companies will exercise the option on your behalf if you miss your deadline, as long as the stock price is higher than the grant price. But don't rely on the kindness of strangers. Treat your options like the volatile assets they are. Keep an eye on them, especially once you're within three years of expiration. And when the moment is ripe, you shouldn't hesitate to cash out and claim your reward. After all, you earned it.

◆ TODAY'S TOP FINANCIAL SUPERMARKETS

There's a war raging on Wall Street for your retirement savings. From giant brokerages like Merrill Lynch to discounters like Charles Schwab, virtually every big company in the business is vying to be your broker, banker, insurance agent and financial planner all rolled into one. The only sure winner in this battle of the titans is individual investors who will have more choices among products and services than ever before, greater convenience and probably lower prices. "Competition is forcing everyone to bring quality up and prices down," says David Pottruck, president of Charles Schwab. "The pressure is on all of us to provide a better deal."

The idea of a financial supermarket is not new. The industry tried and failed to build similar conglomerates in the 1980s. Now Wall Street is embarking on another frenzied round of mergers and expansion. But this time the outcome should be different. A decade ago, the movement was a push from the industry. Today it's a pull from consumers. Still, common sense suggests that no single company can possibly sell the best mutual funds, brokerage services, insurance policies, loans, credit cards and savings accounts. Or offer them all at competitive prices. Moreover, the big firms are rolling out new products and services at such dizzying speed that it's hard to tell the players apart. To help you make sense of it all, MONEY reviewed the offerings of the country's biggest financial supermarkets. We found that there is no single best firm but rather different bests for different investors, depending on which products and services matter most to you.

These giants sell everything financial. Full-service brokerages like Smith Barney and Merrill Lynch and diversified financial services firms like American Express lead the way in offering almost every financial product you could ever desire. Want no-load funds? They've got them. Need a disability policy to go with it? No problem. How about a new mortgage while you're at it? Your Smith Barney broker or American Express planner will be happy to oblige.

Smith Barney was the only firm to offer all 30 items on our checklist, including a complete line of insurance and banking products along with a full range of investments. A close second, Merrill Lynch has 28 of the 30 products (missing only property/casualty insurance and personal loans) but takes top honors for innovations. Among Merrill's more noteworthy bells and whistles is a mortgage program that allows borrowers who use their investments as collateral to forgo a down payment. American Express also boasts 28 out of the 30 items on our checklist. The only gaps in its lineup were new stock issues and futures.

In fact, nearly all the supermarkets we surveyed offered a pretty full complement of investment products. True, some of the upstarts are missing an item or two in the investment exotica category. But even that is changing. Fidelity, for example, can now peddle IPOs (initial public offerings of stock) thanks to its new alliance with Salomon Bros., the investment banking house. A check of some of the supermarkets' noninvestment products, however, suggests that they are rarely the best deals around town. Take mortgages. The six firms on our list that offered them all came in with rates that were pretty much in line with the national averages during the week we checked. But those rates are about three-quarters of a percentage point more than the best deals available nationwide.

The best one-stop fund shopping. For many investors, the greatest appeal of a financial supermarket is its mutual fund marketplace that allows you to use a single account to buy funds from a variety of families. Almost all big full-service brokerages offer one as

FIRM	BREADTH OF PRODUCTS	TRANSACTION PRICES	MUTUAL FUNDS[1] (QUANTITY/QUALITY)
American Express	Rivals full-service brokerages. All types of loans and insurance, plus tax and accounting services. No IPOs or futures. **Grade: A**	Sample trades: $200. All funds are available without a transaction fee. Discounts for online and active traders. **Grade: B**	200 funds from 12 families; 32% are top performers. **Grade: C/B**
Dean Witter	Least extensive lineup of the full-service firms covered. No NTF network, foreign stocks or limited partnerships. Only whole and universal life insurance. **Grade: B**	Sample trades: refused to disclose commissions. Industry surveys suggest prices are somewhat lower than other full-service firms. **Grade: C**	Does not offer no-load funds and has no plans to introduce them. **Grade: F/N.A.**
Dreyfus	No IPOs, foreign bonds, futures or limited partnerships. Mortgages and home-equity lines by year-end. **Grade: C**	Sample trades: $187. Non-NTF funds: $35 for $5,000 fund purchase. Discounts for active traders at broker's discretion. **Grade: B**	543 funds from 60 families; only 26% are top performers. **Grade: B/C**
Fidelity	All investment products except futures. Is introducing term life but offers no other insurance products. Margin loans only. **Grade: B**	Sample trades: $187. Non-NTF funds: $35 for $5,000 fund purchase. Just slashed online fees for active traders to $25 per trade. **Grade: B**	745 funds from 104 families; 31% are top performers. **Grade: A/B**
Merrill Lynch	Second only to Smith Barney in breadth. The gaps: property/casualty insurance and personal loans. Just introduced no-load fund program **Grade: A**	Sample trades: $321. No-load funds available through accounts charging asset-based annual fees. Commission discounts at broker's discretion. **Grade: D**	391 funds from 31 families; 34% are top performers. **Grade: B/B**
Paine Webber	All investments but limited partnerships. Disability and life insurance, but no property/casualty. Margin and personal loans only. **Grade: A**	Sample trades: $213-$283. No-load funds: not available. Commission discounts at broker's discretion. **Grade: C**	No no-load marketplace. A wrap-fee program that includes no-loads is set to debut this fall. **Grade: D/N.A.**

Sources: The companies, Morningstar, Zacks Investment Research and *IBC's Money Fund Report.* **Notes:** NTF stands for no transaction fee, the industry term for mutual fund marketplaces that do not charge a commission on no-load fund transactions. [1]Funds are only those that are available without loads or transaction fees. Scores reflect those funds tracked by Morningstar. N.A. stands for not applicable.

CASH MANAGEMENT	ADVISORY SERVICES	RESEARCH	VARIABLE ANNUITIES
Average rate for taxable money fund, below average for tax-free. Debit and charge cards, plus check writing, direct deposit and electronic bill payment. **Grade: B**	Wide variety of investment and financial planning services from certified planners. Fee-based plans (from $175 to $8,000), as well as wrap programs. **Grade: A**	Free monthly newsletter includes summaries of recommendations from American Express analysts. Other research available. **Grade: B**	One VA has low fees and above-average performance. Two new VAs look promising but are too young to be rated. **Grade: C**
Above-average rate for taxable money fund, average for tax-free. Debit card, check writing and direct deposit. No bill payment and no credit card. **Grade: B**	Free computer-generated financial plans. Fund wrap program for $100,000-plus clients (Dean Witter funds only). Recently introduced fee-based accounts. **Grade: B**	Proprietary picks roughly matched the market over the past one and five years. Outside research at the discretion of individual broker. **Grade: B**	Relatively small selection for a full-service broker. Wide range of fees; mostly subpar performers. **Grade: C**
Average rate for taxable money fund; below average for tax-free. Check writing, debit card, direct deposit and bill payment. No credit card. **Grade: C**	Lion Account ($10,000 minimum) clients get advice from independent planners for $100 a year. Portfolio management for $200,000-plus accounts. **Grade: A**	No proprietary research. Doesn't make other research available to investors either, but "we're working on it." **Grade: D**	One VA that has average expenses and above-average performance. **Grade: B**
High average rates on money funds. Check writing, direct deposit, bill payment and debit card. High-rate credit card. **Grade: A**	General guidance in branch offices and on phone. Portfolio advisory service for $200,000-plus investors, using Fidelity funds only. **Grade: B**	Proprietary research through alliance with Salomon Bros., whose picks beat the market over the past one and five years. Extensive other research available, $2 to $3 per report. **Grade: A**	Relatively low-cost, high-performing product. But recent shake-up in managers of several funds make it difficult to assess prospects. **Grade: B**
Above-average rates on money funds. Low-rate credit card. Debit card, check writing, direct deposit and bill payment. **Grade: A**	Comprehensive basic financial plan: $250. Low minimum ($10,000) fund wrap program; new emerging investor program waives certain minimums. **Grade: B**	Second only to Paine Webber in performance, topping market during past one and five years. **Grade: A**	Nine VAs. Average fees, wide variety in performance. Merrill's own VA is one of the weakest performers. **Grade: C**
Average rates on money-market funds. Debit card but no credit card. Check writing, direct deposit and bill payment. **Grade: B**	Wrap programs (individual securities and Paine Webber funds); launching wrap with expanded mutual fund choices in the fall. **Grade: B**	Winner by a wide margin. Its picks beat the market by six percentage points last year and more than 150 points over the past five. Free outside research. **Grade: A**	16 VAs including most of the big names in the business. Average to high fees, good to average performance. **Grade: B**

FIRM	BREADTH OF PRODUCTS	TRANSACTION PRICES	MUTUAL FUNDS[1] (QUANTITY/QUALITY)
Prudential Securities	All investments but limited partnerships. No credit cards or mortgages, but all other loans. All insurance. **Grade: A**	Sample trades: $287. No-load funds available through accounts charging asset-based fees. Commission discounts at broker's discretion. **Grade: C**	255 funds from 46 families; 44% are top performers. **Grade: B/A**
Quick & Reilly	All investment products except futures and limited partnerships. No insurance or debit card. Margin loans only. **Grade: B**	Sample trades: $139. Non-NTF funds: $25 per transaction. 10% discount on commissions for online and touch-tone phone trading. **Grade: A**	295 funds from 27 families; 31% are top performers. **Grade: B/B**
Charles Schwab	No IPOs, foreign bonds or precious metals. Margin loans only. Last year introduced low-load term and universal life policies. **Grade: B**	Sample trades: $193. Non-NTF funds: $39 for $5,000 purchase. Commission discounts: 10% for touch-tone phone trades; 20% for online traders. **Grade: B**	952 funds from 235 families; 32% are top performers. **Grade: A/B**
Smith Barney	Offers the most complete array of investments, loans and insurance products. **Grade: A**	Sample trades: $283. No-load funds available via asset-based fee program. Commission discounts offered at the broker's discretion. **Grade: C**	81 funds from 28 families; 44% are top performers. **Grade: C/A**
Waterhouse Securities	Mortgages, home-equity lines and other loans. No futures, precious metals or insurance products. **Grade: B**	Sample trades: $95. Non-NTF funds: $25. $12 per online trade up to 5,000 shares. $35 per touch-tone phone trade up to 5,000 shares. **Grade: A**	814 funds from 101 families; 30% are top performers. **Grade: A/B**
Jack White	All investment products except IPOs. Term and universal life insurance only. Margin loans only. Credit card gives 10% discounts on trades. **Grade: B**	Sample trades: $102. Non-NTF funds: $27. 10% discount for touch-tone phone trades; $25 per first 1,250 shares traded online, 2¢ a share thereafter. **Grade: A**	1,104 funds from 171 families; 30% are top performers. **Grade: A/C**

Sources: The companies, Morningstar, Zacks Investment Research and *IBC's Money Fund Report*. **Notes:** NTF stands for no transaction fee, the industry term for mutual fund marketplaces that do not charge a commission on no-load fund transactions. [1]Funds are only those that are available without loads or transaction fees. Scores reflect those funds tracked by Morningstar. N.A. stands for not applicable.

CASH MANAGEMENT	ADVISORY SERVICES	RESEARCH	VARIABLE ANNUITIES
Average rates on money-market funds. Has a debit card but no credit card. Check writing, direct deposit and bill payment. **Grade: B**	Somewhat better-than-average minimums and pricing on wrap programs. Access to independent money managers through fee-based program for $100,000-plus clients. **Grade: B**	Picks up just 13% last year, vs. 21% for market; lagged over five years too. Free outside research. **Grade: B**	Four VAs, all Prudential products. Two are too new to be rated. The other two have average fees, slightly above-average performance. **Grade: B**
Below-average rates on money funds. A middling-rate credit card (around 16%), no debit card, direct deposit or bill payment. **Grade: D**	Educational materials as well as general guidance from personal broker assigned to each client. **Grade: C**	No proprietary research, but extensive outside reports are available, many free, including Morningstar, Value Line and S&P tear sheets. **Grade: B**	Offers seven VAs with average expenses and performance. **Grade: C**
Average rates on money funds. Check writing, direct deposit, bill payment, debit card. Competitive initial rate on credit card. **Grade: B**	Guidance but no outright advice. Computer-generated plans and general help from reps; free referrals offered to fee-based financial advisers. **Grade: B**	No proprietary research. Provides broad range of other research materials including fund picks. Average cost: $1.50 to $3 per report. **Grade: B**	Offers only its own VA. One of the few no-load annuities available, cheap compared with most VAs but too new to be rated. **Grade: N.A.**
Average rates on money funds. Check writing, direct deposit, debit card, bill payment and credit card. **Grade: B**	New comprehensive trading accounts competitively priced at a maximum of 1.5% or 2% of assets ($100,000 minimum). **Grade: B**	Buy recommendations roughly matched market over past one and five years. Free Morningstar and S&P reports. **Grade: B**	Offers 23 VAs with fairly average fees and a wide variety of performance. **Grade: C**
Average rate on taxable money fund, below average on tax-free money fund. Credit card, debit card, check writing, direct deposit, bill payment. **Grade: B**	General guidance from branch managers. No package plans, no personalized advice, no referrals. **Grade: D**	No proprietary research. Free S&P reports and monthly investment newsletter. Morningstar reports (three for $5); discounts on other research and publications. **Grade: B**	Does not currently offer VAs. Set to introduce its own VA series this fall. **Grade: N.A.**
New CMA has near top rates on taxable and tax-free money funds. All other services. **Grade: A**	You're on your own at Jack White: no packaged advice, no general guidance, no referrals. **Grade: F**	No proprietary research. Broad range of other research is available. Average cost: is $1.50 to $3 per report. **Grade: B**	Offers its own VA only. The least expensive VA in the industry, but a subpar performer so far. **Grade: C**

long as you're willing to pay a commission. A more compelling proposition is a so-called NTF (no transaction fee) network, which lets you buy no-loads from different families without paying a commission. Since Schwab pioneered the concept with its One Source program five years ago, the number of NTF programs has exploded. Even full-service firms are getting into the act. But the full-service and discount NTF programs are different animals. First, there's the matter of choice. Four of the five major discount firms get an A for the number of funds they make available without a transaction fee. Here the leader is Jack White with about 1,100 funds. Runners-up Schwab, Waterhouse Securities and Fidelity all weigh in with more than 750 funds. By contrast, the full-service programs have roughly a quarter to half as many funds. The smallest, Smith Barney's No-Load Trak, offers a mere 80 or so funds. At the time of our survey, the Trak funds covered fewer than half the investment categories tracked by fund ranker Morningstar.

What Smith Barney's program lacks in size, however, it makes up in quality. About 45% of the funds in the No-Load Trak program have been in the top 25% of their investment category over the past three years, according to an analysis by Morningstar. That's the best performance of any supermarket on our list. Even better, the funds in Smith Barney's network typically have subpar expense ratios and risk ratings. Prudential's is just as impressive. While these two programs get the only As for quality, Morningstar found that nearly all the supermarkets offer above-average funds. Some 32% of Schwab's One Source funds are in the top quarter, as are 31% of those in Fidelity's network.

The most important difference between the full-service and discount programs is access and price. To qualify for the brokerage fund programs, you have to make at least a five-figure commitment. The minimums range from $10,000 at Merrill to $25,000 at Prudential and Smith Barney. And while it's true that you won't pay the brokerage a transaction fee for your funds, you will be charged an annual fee, ranging from 1% to 1.5% of the amount you've invested, for the asset-allocation advice and specific fund picks that your broker provides.

You also have to determine whether an NTF program offers the particular funds that you want. For example, you can't buy American Century funds without paying a transaction fee through Fidelity. But you can at Schwab. Fidelity, on the other hand, is the only place you can get Fidelity funds without paying a premium. Also check to see the degree of guidance the firm offers if you need help making selections and find out the price for buying funds that are not part of the NTF network. The winners in both of these categories are Quick & Reilly and Waterhouse Securities, which offer a flat $25 fee per transaction.

The lowdown on discount brokers. If paying the lowest commissions on stock trades is paramount, don't shop at the supermarket. Deep-discount firms will almost always give you a better deal. Take the two sample trades we used to compare commissions at the firms we surveyed. To buy 1,000 shares of a $2 stock and 200 shares of a $40 issue, prices ranged from a high total of $321 at Merrill Lynch to a low of $95 at Waterhouse Securities. The same transactions at deep discounter Pacific Brokerage were a mere $58, or roughly 40% less than the cost of trading at the cheapest supermarket and 80% less than the most expensive ones. If you are comfortable going online to make the trades instead, your costs will drop even further. The total bill at E Trade, for example, will run less than $40.

Price wars won't be won on the basis of low commissions, however. Rather, the prize will go to the companies that offer the best combinations of relatively low prices with extensive products and services. By that standard, Waterhouse emerges from the pack. Its commissions were the lowest of any of the firms we surveyed. Yet its offerings were broad, including the third largest NTF network. And its service wins high marks, with an impressive amount of research that's available free or at low cost, nearly 100 branch offices providing general guidance to investors and a personal representative assigned to every account. Low-cost runner-up Jack White, whose rates were just $7 higher than Waterhouse's, has an equally impressive product roster. But the company doesn't offer service extras, guidance, branch offices or personal reps. Taking the opposite path, Schwab and Fidelity are both rapidly expanding their branch systems, their product lines and the degree of guidance that they are willing to offer investors. Their rates are roughly double those at Waterhouse. That's the price you pay for more extensive support and guidance.

The best news for price-conscious investors is that all the competition from deep discounters and online brokers is forcing the old guard to cut prices. Fidelity has introduced a 25% discount for online traders, while Schwab has doubled its online discount from 10% to 20%. But Waterhouse has undercut them all with a flat $12 fee for the first 5,000 shares traded online through June 1998. Even some of the full-service firms are gingerly getting into the act. Merrill Lynch, Prudential and Smith Barney have unveiled new fee-based trading accounts with maximum annual charges of 1.5% or 2% of assets, compared with the maximum 3% fee such wrap programs usually charge.

The best investment advice at a price. Most of the big mutual fund companies and many of the major discounters have decided to invade the full-service shops' turf with portfolio management services and general guidance for investors who manage their own accounts. Unfortunately, it's difficult to rate the quality of advice any of the supermarkets dispense. What we were able to assess was the breadth and cost of advisory options each supermarket delivers. American Express and Dreyfus earn As for innovative new programs that offer ongoing counsel to both small and large investors at competitive prices. Through its Financial Direct program, American Express gives do-it-yourselfers solid support through a quarterly investment newsletter, a list of recommended funds and free telephone consultations with licensed brokers. Through its Financial Advisors service, American Express also provides one-time planning as well as money management for annual fees ranging from 0.5% to 3% of assets.

Dreyfus offers a similarly impressive array of advisory services through its Lion Account and Masterpiece programs. For a minimum investment of $10,000 and an annual fee of $100 a year, Lion customers get access to unlimited telephone counseling from independent financial planners. For investors with at least $200,000 in assets, Dreyfus also provides money management, charging a maximum of 1.1% of assets a year. Unlike similar programs by competitors, the recommendations include outside products as well as Dreyfus' own funds.

Full-service brokerages, of course, have the clear edge when it comes to specific stock recommendations. Most discounters and fund companies don't even offer proprietary research. But you can expect mixed results, according to Zacks Investment Research, a Chicago firm that assesses the performance of stocks recommended by Wall Street's major research departments. Over recent one- and five-year periods, Smith Barney's research department managed only to match the market's performance. Prudential fared worse, lagging the market by eight percentage points over the past year and underperforming over the five-year period too. Paine Webber, we discovered, is the clear standout in research. Its stock recommendations gained 27% last year, compared with 21% for the Wilshire 5000, and a stunning 252% over the past five years, vs. 100% for the market. Now that's advice worth taking.

◆ MAKE THE MOST OF YOUR BROKER

Under extreme pressure to meet their commission goals, stockbrokers don't always do what's best for their clients. That, at least, is the view of Mark Dempsey. He spent almost three years selling stocks and bonds for one of Wall Street's biggest brokerage firms until June 1995, when he was let go for refusing to meet sales goals he called unfair. Today he runs a financial consulting business in Dallas, advising investors about how to manage their accounts and protect their interests. Below Dempsey describes the most common mistakes investors make in dealing with their broker.

The most important investment tip. "Don't trust your broker 100%," says Dempsey. "I say that with insider knowledge because for nearly three years I was a successful broker in Dallas. Within my first two years, my bosses expected me to amass $10 million in assets, open 150 accounts and generate $150,000 in commissions. I did just that. How? By becoming a supersalesman rather than a first-rate investment adviser." One thing he learned: "While I couldn't rely on the market to go up or down, I could always rely on my clients to make the same mistakes over and over. Now that I'm out of the business, I'm free to tell you the ways you can come out on top when dealing with your broker, as well as things you should do when choosing a new one."

Always ask for a discount. "You can get price breaks on your stock trades. At my firm, I could discount up to 35% without management approval and waive certain customer account fees altogether. This kind of flexibility is common at full-service brokerages. But you might never know about it. When clients balked about their fees, I would generally tell them that you get what you pay for. Not true! Always ask your broker for a discount and think big. Ask for 50% off the stated commission and then negotiate a compromise."

Make your broker pay attention to you. "One day at a monthly sales meeting, a fellow broker asked how we manage our smaller accounts. The sales manager stood up and gave the correct answer. 'We don't.' To commission-hungry brokers, bigger portfolios are almost always better. So if your portfolio is chickenfeed compared with your broker's other accounts, you could get hurt. Here's the corollary. Brokers focus more attention on clients who demand it than they do on clients who don't. The lesson? If you're not a big wheel, be a squeaky one."

Note the cutoff date for sales goals. "Most firms pay brokers once a month based on how much they've generated in commissions. As the cutoff date for meeting commission goals approaches, commission-motivated trading increases. An academic study that scrutinized the trading records of 100 Wall Street brokers revealed that 29 consistently earned a significantly higher portion of their commission income during the last full week of the month. Seven earned 40% or more of their commissions in the last full week of the month. Be wary of recommendations your broker makes to you at this time."

Let your comfort level be your guide. "My office manager was fond of the 'ask till they gasp' maneuver. A broker would propose that a client buy so many shares of stock that he'd gasp. Then the broker would back off with a recommendation for a slightly lower number of shares. This technique lets a broker quickly learn your tolerance level so that he can sell you as much as possible. Always let your own comfort level and investment needs, not your broker's commission goals, determine how many shares of stock you buy."

Pick a broker based on research. "C.P.A.s, lawyers and other professionals tend to be a broker's biggest source of referrals. Yet they often know very little about the broker they're recommending. One C.P.A. referred his clients to me after knowing me for only two days. In another case, a local attorney talked me up to his clients shortly after I promised to pass on some of my clients to him. Before doing business with a broker, always visit him at his office so you can form your own impressions. And check him or her out thoroughly for complaints filed by other clients. Also be sure to ask your broker for evidence in writing of his professional credentials." [Note: call the National Association of Securities Dealers (800-289-9999) to obtain a report listing any disciplinary actions, criminal convictions and arbitration decisions against a broker. The NASD also provides data on pending complaints or arbitration cases that allege damages of $5,000 or more plus settlements involving payments of $10,000 and up.]

Just say no to cold calls. "I spent hundreds of dollars on lists of prospects whom I cold called with a special offer. My offer was rarely special. And accepting it was always a bad idea for the same reason it's a bad idea to listen to a psychiatrist on the radio. The advice is given without knowing you. To reduce the number of unsolicited calls you get, tell the broker to put your name on the firm's do-not-call list. Then send the request in writing to the broker's compliance manager to make sure that it's honored."

◆ THE SCOOP ON FEE-ONLY PLANNERS

People nearing or entering retirement have heard this advice again and again. If you need a financial planner, look for one who gets paid solely by charging fees for his or her services. Such fee-only planners don't earn commissions from the products they recommend. Thus there's no built-in conflict between your financial interest and theirs. A MONEY study, however, has concluded that the conventional wisdom may no longer be so wise. You should indeed use only a planner with no conflicts of interest. But our reporting, which included a close examination of more than 100 financial planning firms in five states, revealed that such planners are very difficult to turn up.

Consider, for example, that nearly a third of the planners who had assured our undercover reporters they were fee-only actually take commissions for selling securities or insurance, according to documents filed with securities regulators. And a troubling 13% of the planning firms we examined have had brushes with the law. Yet only 43% of the fee-only advisers we studied had earned any of the professional designations that signify training in financial planning. Anyone can call himself a planner.

To be sure, many fee-only planners provide solid advice and carefully avoid conflicts of interest. But our investigation shows you can no longer assume that planners who call themselves fee-only are legit until you've checked their training, compensation and disciplinary record.

How financial planners operate. A good one can provide sound advice on everything from insurance and investments to taxes and retirement. The planner will review your total financial picture and suggest a strategy tailored to your resources, your goals and your attitude toward investment risk. He will also help you put the plan into action and update it as your needs change. Planners are paid for their services in one of three ways. Fee-only advisers charge a flat amount for a financial plan, typically $500 to $6,000, depending on the complexity of your affairs. Or they charge an hourly fee ranging from $75 to $225. Many also assess annual charges that are equal to 0.5% to 1.5% of your assets to manage your money on a continuing basis. Commission-based planners earn most of their income from commissions on the mutual funds, insurance policies and other financial products that they sell to their clients. Fee-based planners are hybrids who receive both fees and commissions.

Consumer advocates insist that true fee-only planning is best for most people. They argue that it doesn't eliminate every conflict. But it comes closer than any other arrangement. As a result, fee-only has become the field's fastest growing segment. Baby boomers, according to numerous surveys, are more willing than their parents to pay for advice. With so many mutual funds and annuities to chose among, even knowledgeable investors often need help sorting through their options. And as the population ages, retirement planning has become a more urgent priority for many Americans.

At the same time, brokerage and investment companies, such as Charles Schwab and Fidelity, have made it far easier for planners to set up and run fee-only practices. Through those firms, planners can buy and sell no-load funds for their clients (as well as funds that carry commissions). Schwab and Fidelity also provide special services, such as statements that consolidate all of a customer's holdings. Not to be left behind, Federated, T. Rowe Price, Vanguard and other fund companies have created departments to answer fee-only and fee-based planners' questions and provide them with services like customized reports and meetings with fund experts.

What our planner probe found. We asked Money Market Directories, a Charlottesville, Va. financial publisher, for a list of investment advisers in the Boston, Chicago, Dallas, Los Angeles and Miami areas. A MONEY reporter then called each firm and, posing as a small investor, asked whether its planners worked on a fee-only basis. We also checked the Yellow Pages in those cities for people who advertised themselves as fee-only planners. If the firm said it was fee-only, we next asked the state's securities regulators for a copy of the firm's registration form, which details its planners' compensation arrangements, experience, past legal problems and potential conflicts of interest. We also asked regulators to check the Central Registration Depository (CRD), a computer database that tracks brokers, for any legal actions involving the firms.

We found that many people who claim to be fee-only planners aren't. Thirty-eight of the 109 firms that assured us they were fee-only say on their registration forms that they accept commissions or receive referral fees from money managers. In some cases, a planning firm may have changed its practices since filing the registration form. In others, the firm may work with a few longtime customers on a commission basis but charge most new clients only fees. But other firms appear to derive a substantial amount of income from commissions. "Many people say they're fee-only because they don't count insurance or any securities that carry commissions," says David Diesslin of the National Association of Personal Financial Advisors, which limits its membership to planners who receive all compensation in fees.

How to check out a planner's past. A little-known document called Form ADV is one of the best sources of information about a financial planner's history, qualifications and potential conflicts of interest. Most planners are required to file an ADV with federal regulators and to submit the same form or a similar one to their state securities department. A planner must give you either Part II of the ADV or a brochure that answers the same questions at your first meeting. If the planner gives you a brochure, insist on the ADV. That's because it's harder for a planner to gloss over troublesome details in the form. Also ask for Part I of the ADV, which the planner is not required to give you but usually will on request. It discloses any legal or financial troubles the planner may have had. There's a caveat, however. Not everything a planner says on the ADV may be true. Although some states scrutinize ADVs more thoroughly, the federal Securities and Exchange Commission checks only for contradictions in the document and verifies whether the planner has been forthright about past legal problems. That said, here are the four key areas of the ADV you should examine closely before hiring a planner.

◆ **Legal and financial problems** (Part I, questions 11A through K). A yes answer to any of these questions means the planner has had legal or regulatory problems or has done a poor job of managing his own finances. Ask the planner to explain any yesses. However compelling his excuses may be, you probably don't want to do business with a planner whose form shows a pattern of past problems.

◆ **Compensation** (Part II, questions 1C, 1D, 13A, and Schedule F). The answers here will tell you how the planner is paid. If the planner doesn't say he receives commissions in question 1C, be sure to check Schedule F. We found lots of cases where planners acknowledged only in this appendix–most likely in violation of the law–that they received commissions. Avoid planners whose total costs, including any fees, mutual fund expenses and custodial charges, equal 2% or more of the value of your portfolio.

◆ **Education and business background** (Part II, question 6, and Schedule F). Look for a planner who has at least five years of experience and a professional designation such as certified financial planner (C.F.P.), certified public accountant–personal financial specialist (C.P.A.–P.F.S.), chartered financial consultant (Ch.F.C.) or chartered life underwriter (C.L.U.). If a planner describes himself as a "registered representative," that's a tip-off he is a salesman who receives commissions.

◆ **Other business affiliations** (Part II, questions 7 and 8, and Schedule F). Watch out for signs of potential conflicts of interest. These include ties to a broker-dealer or an insurance company, referral fees from money managers and limited partnerships that the adviser both runs and sells to his planning clients.

How to pick a talented planner. First decide what kind of help you need. A fee-only adviser may be your best choice, particularly if you want a comprehensive financial checkup. But if you find fee-only planners too pricey or have only a small amount to invest and want help choosing mutual funds, you might consider a planner who accepts both fees and commissions–and is up front about it. These steps can help you find a capable planner. Interview several candidates before settling on a final choice.

◆ **Get recommendations.** Ask local lawyers, accountants and bank trust officers for the names of reputable planners. You can also request referrals from these groups: the International Association for Financial Planning (800-945-4237), the Institute of Certified Financial Planners (800-282-7526), the National Association of Personal Financial Advisors (800-366-2732), the American Institute of Certified Public Accountants–Personal Financial Planning Division (800-862-4272) and the American Society of Chartered Life Underwriters and Chartered Financial Consultants (800-392-6900).

◆ **Make sure the planner is registered.** Most are required to register with the SEC. In all but four states (Colorado, Iowa, Ohio and Wyoming), planners usually must file with their state securities departments. Registration isn't a governmental seal of approval. But it does mean the planner has filled out a federal or state form disclosing his experience. You also can check whether there's a regulatory rap sheet. Your state securities regulator should be able to tell you if it has any complaints or legal actions pending against a planner. If he has ever worked as a stockbroker, ask your state securities regulator or the National Association of Securities Dealers (800-289-9999) whether the planner has been disciplined for ethical or legal violations.

◆ **Ask for references.** Ask each candidate to provide you with the names of people with financial circumstances similar to yours who have been clients for at least three years. Be sure to ask them whether the planner has given them their money's worth.

◆ **Get it in writing.** Once you've picked a planner, you should promptly ask for what's called an engagement letter or service agreement. It should detail how much you'll have to pay and what you can expect in return.

◆ WHY VARIABLE ANNUITIES ARE HOT

Insurance agents, stockbrokers, financial planners and bankers are busy pushing their own version of a tax cut plan. Their pitch? Shave your IRS bill by investing in a tax-deferred variable annuity. While annuities are sponsored by life insurance companies, they're not quite as bewildering as they might seem at first glance. Variable annuities surround fundlike portfolios called subaccounts with a thin layer of insurance protection. These subaccounts often are run by well-known fund companies such as Dreyfus, Fidelity and Vanguard. They typically require a minimum initial investment of $500 to $5,000 with the flexibility to add to your account whenever you wish.

The money you invest grows tax deferred until you withdraw it, just as it would in an IRA or 401(k) plan. When you pull out your cash from the annuity, you pay ordinary income taxes on any gains plus a 10% penalty on any withdrawals made before age 59.5. There's no limit, however, on how much you can sock away each year in an annuity. That's because you invest after-tax dollars, not the pretax money you can stash in a 401(k) or the tax-deductible contribution you may be able to make with an IRA. Another drawback of variable annuities is that you should be willing to lock away your cash for at least 10 years. Otherwise, the thicket of fees that you will face could help wipe out those highly touted tax breaks.

If you decide that variables are a worthwhile addition to your portfolio, you'll want to consult MONEY's rankings beginning on page 122 that identify the 15 top performers among the hundreds of annuities tracked by Morningstar. For investors who prefer to tilt their retirement portfolio toward a particular style, the table "Your Best Choices for Specific Goals" on page 129 lists the annuities whose growth, total return, bond or international stock subaccounts posted the best performance. Annuities with stars next to their names on our top 15 list excelled in our overall rankings and made our list of best performers for specific investment aims as well.

How variable annuities work. A typical one lets you divvy up your money among seven or more subaccounts that include a wide range of asset classes, such as domestic and international stocks and government and corporate bonds. If you are a hands-off investor, you can set an initial allocation and then leave your account untouched so that your gains compound free of taxes until you withdraw them. If you prefer switching your money among the annuity's subaccounts, you can do so without having to pay taxes on any capital gains you generate. By contrast, switch from one mutual fund to another, and you could owe taxes.

You can't talk about variables without discussing their fees, fees and more fees. All variables carry a so-called annual insurance cost, which averages about 1.25% of assets. This levy helps pay sales commissions, other marketing expenses and the cost of providing a death benefit. It promises that your beneficiaries will receive at least the principal you invested over the years, regardless of the performance of your subaccounts. Add in the cost of managing those subaccount portfolios, typically 0.82% a year, and a variable's annual expenses can easily lumber in at 2% or more, vs. an average of 1.4% for stock mutual funds overall. On top of that, you'll probably be hit up for an additional yearly contract charge of $25 to $40.

As if all those expenses weren't enough, most variables also tack on a surrender charge equal to 5% to 9% of the money you withdraw within the first five to 10 years. (Many let you pull out 10% of your principal or account balance each year without triggering this penalty.) Similar to the back-end load on some mutual funds, the surrender charge declines from the maximum by a percentage point or so each year until it disappears.

Who should invest in variables. Since their steep fees cut into your net returns, variables should never be your first choice for retirement investing. Says Jennifer Strickland of Morningstar: "We recommend you consider annuities only after you've maxed out your contributions to 401(k), IRA and other tax-deferred accounts." Similarly, because it takes years of tax-deferred compounding to overcome the drag of fees, you shouldn't buy a variable unless you're in at least the 28% federal tax bracket.

How we picked the top performers. Still game? One of our top 15 variable annuities may be right for you. To make our list, these annuities had to beat their peers over a period of at least three years in a minimum of three broad investing categories–growth, total return and bonds. We considered only those top performers that are available in a majority of states, let you make contributions whenever you want (as opposed to a single lump sum) and offer at least one subaccount in three investment categories. Each subaccount was graded on its three-year investment performance (net of annual insurance charges and subaccount expenses) relative to its competitors on a scale of 100 (best) to 1 (worst). If a subaccount had a five-year record, we factored in its performance over that period as well. Subaccounts that did not have at least a three-year record were not included in our analysis. For instance, the Life of Virginia Commonwealth VA Plus offers a total of 27 different

Propelled by robust returns from its three subaccounts and below-average fees, Mass Mutual Panorama vaulted to the top of our list of best-performing variable annuities. Runner-up Vanguard Variable Annuity Plan features five more investment options and even lower fees than Panorama but was dragged down by subpar returns in one subaccount. To learn how we ranked the annuities, see the methodology section below. The numbered boxes list key details such as each annuity's contract charge and surrender fee. Annuities with stars next to their names also appear in the table on page 129 that lists top performers in four specific investment categories.

Methodology: To be ranked, an annuity had to be available in a majority of states, accept periodic investments and offer at least one subaccount with a three-year or longer track record in each of three broad categories: growth (including growth and aggressive growth subaccounts), total return (including balanced, growth and income, and specialty subaccounts such as real estate or utilities) and fixed income (including corporate, government and high-yield bond subaccounts). If an annuity had international stock or bond accounts, we considered them too. We then asked Morningstar to assign each subaccount a score from 100 (best) to 1 (worst) based on its percentile performance compared with other subaccounts that have the same investment objective during a recent three-year period or a weighted average of recent three- and five-year periods. Finally, we averaged the scores of individual subaccounts to produce each annuity's overall score and rank.

Notes: Some annuities may waive the minimum initial investment if you agree to invest, say, $50 or more each month; some also waive the contract charge if your account balance tops a specified figure, usually $25,000 or more. [1]Type: AG: aggressive growth; B: balanced; CB: corporate bond; G: growth; GB: government bond; GI: growth and income; HY: high-yield bond; IB: international bond; IS: international stock; SP: specialty fund; [2]Subaccount expense ratios reflect actual costs charged to investors for the most recent full year (1995), as a percentage of assets. [3]Morningstar risk ratings range from 1 (lowest risk) to 5 (highest risk) and measure a subaccount's volatility as compared with that of others in its category. [4]Total returns are net of all fees except surrender fees and annual contract charge. [5]This reflects the insurance cost in effect until May 1996; the charge is now 0.46%. [6]The company offers a similar annuity with more investment choices but slightly different terms under the name The Best of America IV/Nationwide. [7]Dreyfus/Transamerica Triple Advantage

| SUBACCOUNT NAME | TYPE[1] | EXPENSE RATIO[2] | RISK RATING[3] | % ANNUALIZED RETURN[4] | | SUBACCOUNT SCORE |
				THREE YEARS	FIVE YEARS	
1. MASS MUTUAL PANORAMA ★			**800-234-5606**			
Total funds: 4	Min. initial investment: $500		Contract charge: $40			
Insurance cost: 0.73%	Top surrender fee: 5%		Expires: 10th year			
Panorama Growth	G	0.66%	3	13.4	16.0	86
Panorama Total Return	B	0.59	2	7.8	11.1	81
Panorama Income	CB	0.65	3	3.1	7.0	77
2. VANGUARD VARIABLE ANNUITY ★			**800-523-9954**			
Total funds: 9	Min. initial investment: $5,000		Contract charge: $25			
Insurance cost: 0.48%[5]	Top surrender fee: none					
Vanguard Growth	G	0.47%	1	17.8	N.A.	97
Vanguard Balanced	B	0.36	3	11.3	11.5	95
Vanguard Equity Index	GI	0.28	2	14.2	12.7	76
Vanguard High-Grade Bond	CB	0.29	3	3.9	6.6	76
Vanguard Equity Income	GI	0.39	1	12.0	N.A.	27

SUBACCOUNT NAME	TYPE[1]	EXPENSE RATIO[2]	RISK RATING[3]	% ANNUALIZED RETURN[4]		SUBACCOUNT SCORE
				THREE YEARS	FIVE YEARS	
3. FIDELITY RETIREMENT RESERVES			**800-544-2442**			
Total funds: 10	Min. initial investment: $2,500		Contract charge: $30			
Insurance cost: 1%	Top surrender fee: 5%		Expires: 5th year			
Fidelity High Income	HY	0.71%	1	9.6	14.3	96
Fidelity Equity-Income	GI	0.61	2	13.4	15.3	93
Fidelity Index 500	GI	0.28	2	13.6	N.A.	91
Fidelity Growth	G	0.70	4	12.2	14.4	72
Fidelity Inv. Grade Bond	CB	0.59	2	3.0	6.1	55
Fidelity Asset Manager	B	0.79	3	5.9	8.9	50
Fidelity Overseas	IS	0.91	3	6.2	7.4	38
4. OPPENHEIMER FUNDS LIFETRUST			**800-525-7048**			
Total funds: 13	Min. initial investment: $2,000		Contract charge: $30			
Insurance cost: 1.4%	Top surrender fee: 7%		Expires: 7th year			
Oppenheimer Strat. Bond	CB	0.85%	2	5.1	N.A.	92
Oppenheimer Growth	G	0.79	1	15.2	14.1	77
Oppenheimer Multi.-Strat.	B	0.77	2	8.4	9.9	77
Oppenheimer Bond	CB	0.80	2	3.8	6.5	72
MML Blend	B	0.38	1	8.6	9.3	71
Oppenheimer Global Secs.	IS	0.89	4	6.4	9.5	59
MML Managed Bond	CB	0.52	4	2.8	6.1	51
Oppenheimer High Income	HY	0.81	1	8.1	12.8	50
MML Equity	GI	0.41	1	12.3	11.6	29
5. BANKERS SECURITY USA PLAN			**800-595-7827**			
Total funds: 19	Min. initial investment: $1,000		Contract charge: $30			
Insurance cost: 1.25%	Top surrender fee: 7%		Expires: 8th year			
Oppenheimer Strat. Bond	CB	0.85%	2	5.2	N.A.	95
Fidelity Index 500	GI	0.28	2	13.3	N.A.	85
Oppenheimer Multi.-Strat.	B	0.77	2	8.5	10.0	80
Fidelity Equity-Income	GI	0.61	2	13.1	15.0	80
Oppenheimer Growth	G	0.79	1	15.0	14.0	74
Oppenheimer Cap. Apprec.	AG	0.78	5	14.9	17.3	72
Fidelity Growth	G	0.70	4	11.9	14.1	65
Oppenheimer Global Secs.	IS	0.89	4	6.5	9.6	61
Oppenheimer High Income	HY	0.81	1	8.8	13.2	56
Fidelity Asset Manager	B	0.79	3	5.8	8.8	47
Alliance Growth & Income	GI	0.79	2	12.8	10.6	25
Alliance S/T Multi-Market	IB	0.95	3	0.9	1.8	18

SUBACCOUNT NAME	TYPE[1]	EXPENSE RATIO[2]	RISK RATING[3]	% ANNUALIZED RETURN[4]		SUBACCOUNT SCORE
				THREE YEARS	FIVE YEARS	
6. OHIO NATIONAL TOP B ★				800-366-6654		
Total funds: 9 Min. initial investment: $25				Contract charge: $30		
Insurance cost: 1.1% Top surrender fee: 8%				Expires: 8th year		
Ohio National Intl.	IS	1.12%	1	12.3	N.A.	91
Ohio National Omni	B	0.75	2	8.6	9.8	78
Ohio National Bond	CB	0.75	3	2.9	6.0	51
Ohio National Equity	G	0.73	2	11.1	10.8	33
7. MONY MASTER ★				800-487-6669		
Total funds: 9 Min. initial investment: $2,000				Contract charge: $30		
Insurance cost: 1.25% Top surrender fee: 7%				Expires: 8th year		
Enterprise Managed	B	0.67%	3	16.7	17.1	98
Enterprise Equity	G	0.69	2	16.0	15.7	93
MONY Long Term Bond	CB	0.48	5	2.8	7.4	73
MONY I/T Bond	CB	0.49	1	3.1	5.4	34
Enterprise Small Cap	AG	0.69	3	6.4	11.7	6
8. MULTI-FLEX IV/NATIONWIDE[6]				800-243-6295		
Total funds: 5 Min. initial investment: $1,500				Contract charge: $30		
Insurance cost: 1.3% Top surrender fee: 7%				Expires: 7th year		
Nationwide Gov. Bond	GB	0.51%	3	2.8	6.1	74
Nationwide Cap. Apprec.	G	0.54	1	13.4	N.A.	73
Nationwide Total Return	GI	0.51	1	10.9	12.0	34
9. SCUDDER HORIZON PLAN				800-225-2470		
Total funds: 7 Min. initial investment: $2,500				Contract charge: $0		
Insurance cost: 0.7% Top surrender fee: none						
Scudder Balanced	B	0.65%	3	8.8	9.5	76
Scudder International	IS	1.08	3	8.2	9.7	73
Scudder Bond	CB	0.56	4	2.6	6.8	61
Scudder Capital Growth	G	0.57	3	8.4	11.2	28
10. PUTNAM CAPITAL MANAGER				800-521-0538		
Total funds: 11 Min. initial investment: $1,000				Contract charge: $30		
Insurance cost: 1.4% Top surrender fee: 6%				Expires: 7th year		
PCM Voyager	AG	0.68%	3	16.2	16.4	73
PCM Global Asset Alloc.	B	0.84	2	8.1	9.4	69
PCM Global Growth	IS	0.75	3	8.7	9.4	68
PCM Growth & Income	GI	0.57	2	13.1	12.0	53
PCM Utilities Gro. & Inc.	SP	0.68	2	6.3	N.A.	51
PCM Gov./High Qual. Bond	CB	0.70	4	2.6	6.4	50
PCM High Yield	HY	0.79	1	8.3	12.2	47

| SUBACCOUNT NAME | TYPE[1] | EXPENSE RATIO[2] | RISK RATING[3] | % ANNUALIZED RETURN[4] | | SUBACCOUNT SCORE |
				THREE YEARS	FIVE YEARS	
11. GENERAL AMER. SEP. ACCT. 2			**800-449-6447**			
Total funds: 8	Min. initial investment: $300		Contract charge: $0			
Insurance cost: 1%	Top surrender fee: 9%		Expires: 9th year			
Fidelity Equity-Income	GI	0.61%	2	13.4	15.3	94
Fidelity Growth	G	0.70	4	12.2	14.4	72
Gen. Amer. S&P 500 Index	GI	0.32	3	13.6	12.2	68
General Amer. Asset Alloc.	B	0.60	2	8.7	8.7	64
General Amer. Bond Index	CB	0.30	3	2.8	5.9	48
Fidelity Overseas	IS	0.91	3	6.2	7.4	39
General Amer. Man. Equity	G	0.52	2	11.3	9.4	25
12. DREYFUS/TRANSAMER. TR. ADV.[7] ★			**800-258-4260**			
Total funds: 13	Min. initial investment: $5,000		Contract charge: $30			
Insurance cost: 1.4%	Top surrender fee: 6%		Expires: 7th year			
Dreyfus Small Cap	AG	0.83%	3	19.5	40.6	88
Dreyfus Cap. Appreciation	G	0.85	1	14.6	N.A.	85
Dreyfus Quality Bond	CB	0.81	4	2.7	8.0	74
Dreyfus Zero Coupon 2000	GB	0.68	3	2.5	7.6	71
Dreyfus Stock Index	GI	0.40	2	12.9	11.5	32
Dreyfus Managed Assets	B	0.94	3	1.8	5.9	1
13. LIFE OF VA. COMMONWEALTH PLUS			**800-388-8966**			
Total funds: 27	Min. initial investment: $5,000		Contract charge: $25			
Insurance cost: 1.4%	Top surrender fee: 6%		Expires: 6th year			
LOV Total Return	B	0.65%	1	9.5	10.2	85
Alger Growth	G	0.85	4	14.3	14.9	84
Oppenheimer Multi.-Strat.	B	0.77	1	8.8	10.1	83
Oppenheimer Cap. Apprec.	AG	0.78	4	15.9	18.2	80
Oppenheimer Growth	G	0.79	1	15.1	14.0	75
Oppenheimer Bond	CB	0.80	2	3.7	6.5	71
LOV Common Stock Index	GI	0.66	1	13.3	12.7	70
Fidelity Equity-Income	GI	0.61	2	12.9	14.8	62
Fidelity Growth	G	0.70	4	11.8	14.0	53
Oppenheimer High Income	HY	0.81	1	8.1	12.8	50
Alger Small Cap	AG	0.92	5	12.6	13.2	37
Fidelity Asset Manager	B	0.79	3	5.4	8.5	28
Fidelity Overseas	IS	0.91	3	5.7	7.0	16
LOV Government Secs.	GB	0.74	4	1.0	4.8	7

| SUBACCOUNT NAME | TYPE[1] | EXPENSE RATIO[2] | RISK RATING[3] | % ANNUALIZED RETURN[4] | | SUBACCOUNT SCORE |
				THREE YEARS	FIVE YEARS	
14. NYLIAC VARIABLE ANNUITY			**800-598-2019**			
Total funds: 11	Min. initial investment: $2,500		Contract charge: $30			
Insurance cost: 1.3%	Top surrender fee: 7%		Expires: 9th year			
NY Life Total Return	B	0.69%	3	8.0	N.A.	70
NY Life Indexed Equity	GI	0.47	2	12.9	N.A.	55
NY Life Government	GB	0.67	2	2.6	N.A.	53
NY Life Capital Apprec.	G	0.73	3	11.9	N.A.	50
15. TRAVELERS UNIVERSAL ANNUITY			**800-842-9368**			
Total funds: 29	Min. initial investment: $1,000		Contract charge: $30			
Insurance cost: 1.25%	Top surrender fee: 5%		Expires: 5th year			
Templeton Stock	IS	0.66%	3	12.4	14.3	95
Templeton Asset Alloc.	B	0.66	3	9.8	12.1	94
Fidelity High Income	HY	0.71	1	9.3	14.0	94
Am. Odyssey Intl. Equity	IS	1.08	4	10.6	N.A.	84
Am. Odyssey Emerging Opp.	AG	0.77	5	18.2	N.A.	82
Fidelity Equity-Income	GI	0.61	2	13.1	15.0	79
Am. Odyssey S/T Bond	GB	0.77	1	2.9	N.A.	69
Fidelity Growth	G	0.70	4	11.9	14.2	66
Travelers Quality Bond	CB	0.32	1	3.7	6.3	64
Travelers Capital Apprec.	AG	0.85	3	13.3	15.2	62
Am. Odyssey I/T Bond	CB	0.75	2	2.8	N.A.	56
Templeton Bond	IB	0.78	3	3.1	6.1	47
Dreyfus Stock Index	GI	0.40	2	13.0	11.6	41
Travelers Managed Assets	B	0.58	2	7.6	8.3	41
Travelers U.S. Gov. Secs.	GB	0.56	5	2.5	N.A.	40
Fidelity Asset Manager	B	0.79	3	5.6	8.6	39
Am. Odyssey L/T Bond	CB	0.70	5	2.6	N.A.	35
Travelers Growth & Inc.	GI	0.45	2	13.0	10.8	32
Am. Odyssey Core Equity	GI	0.70	2	11.9	N.A.	26
Travelers High Yield Bond	HY	1.25	1	7.4	10.3	25
Travelers Social Awareness	G	1.25	2	10.3	N.A.	24

variable subaccounts. But we graded it solely on the 14 with a three-year or longer record. We then averaged those subaccount grades to award the annuity an overall score. We didn't include the performance of fixed-rate or money-market subaccounts in our rankings because, we believe, variable annuity investors ought to focus their long-term strategy on higher-gaining growth and bond investments.

Our winner is Mass Mutual Panorama, which distinguished itself with outstanding top-quartile performance in all three subaccounts we graded. For example, portfolio manager Peter Antos, who also manages the well-regarded Oppenheimer Disciplined Value mutual fund, steered Panorama Growth to average annual gains of 16% over five years. That whipped 85% of its competitors. Antos also heads up the four-person management team for Panorama Total Return, which topped 80% of its peers with an 11% annualized return. At least part of the annuity's stellar performance also stems from its below-average fees. Panorama's 0.73% insurance charge is well below its peers' average of 1.25%.

Vanguard Variable Annuity Plan placed second with solid performance from four of the five subaccounts we graded. Vanguard Growth, managed by Parker Hall and David Fowler, beat 96% of its growth competitors with a three-year return of almost 18% annually. Hall and Fowler also manage the Vanguard U.S. Growth mutual fund, which ranks in the top 10% of growth funds for the past three years and, like the annuity subaccount, focuses on large-company growth stocks. The Vanguard annuity is notable for ultralow expenses. Its insurance charge, which declines as assets increase, recently dropped from 0.48% to 0.46%, or roughly 60% below the industry average. The Vanguard annuity is one of the few variable annuities that levies no surrender charges. Rounding out the top trio is Fidelity Retirement Reserves led by strong showings from both its bond and equity income subaccounts. While any of the top performers on our list might be right for you, here are additional factors to consider before choosing an annuity.

Pick a range of investments. Most annuity investors should focus on ones that have strong stock subaccounts. That's because only stocks are capable of returning 10% to 12% annually over periods of a decade or longer. Finding annuities that excel in growth investing won't be difficult. Our top three scorers, Mass Mutual Panorama, Vanguard Variable Annuity Plan and Fidelity Retirement Reserves, all offer domestic stock options that have topped at least 70% of their peers. To lower the volatility that comes with U.S. stocks, however, you'll probably want to diversify your holdings with other types of subaccounts, such as international funds and portfolios that invest in government or corporate bonds.

As you scan our overall winners list, check to see whether the annuity contains the full spectrum of investment objectives that you would like to include in your account. To get the diversity you need, you might have to look beyond the annuities at the top of our rankings. No. 1 Mass Mutual Panorama, for example, offers no international fund or high-yield bond fund. You can switch annuities without incurring taxes by making a so-called 1035 tax-free exchange. But you could still be whacked with hefty surrender charges on money you've invested in recent years.

Focus on investing, not on insurance.
Beware of marketing pitches that tout gimmicky features such as a stepped-up death benefit that resets the benefit periodically to the higher of the account's market value or what you have paid in. Some annuities, such as Dreyfus/Transamerica Triple Advantage, have a step-up plus other options. They promise to pay your beneficiaries the principal you invested plus 5% in annual interest or the current market value of your annuity, whichever is higher. But these features can boost the insurance charge by two-tenths of a percentage point or so. And they don't offer much in the way of worthwhile protection. That's because the death benefit is paid out only if your account's value is down from the last reset and you happen to die at that time. It's possible but unlikely. Therefore, to get protection you'll probably never use, you are accepting higher expenses and thus lower returns. So don't fall for the insurance protection hook. Instead, choose an annuity using the same investment savvy you would when picking a mutual fund.

Look for low-cost options.
Everything else being equal, the higher your annuity's fees, the less cash you'll have when you're ready to start pulling out money from your account. But don't automatically jump at the lowest-cost option. After all, it may be worth it to pay a little more for a wider selection of subaccounts or access to a top-performing subaccount. As with car buying, the key is to shop for the best price for the options you want. You may well find that two variable annuities have the same subaccounts but with vastly different fees. For example, buy the Fidelity Growth and Fidelity Equity-Income sub-

♦ Your Best Choices for Specific Goals

These variable annuities topped one or more of four investment categories. A few, like Mass Mutual Panorama and MONY Master, made our overall winners list too.

	PHONE	SCORE[1]
GROWTH		
GT Global Allocator	800-237-6580	98
Vanguard Variable Annuity Plan	800-523-9954	97
Sierra Advantage	800-531-6466	92
USAA Life Variable Annuity	800-531-6390	89
Dreyfus/Transamer. Triple Advan.	800-258-4260	86
Mass Mutual Panorama	800-234-5606	86
TOTAL RETURN		
MONY Master	800-487-6669	98
Templeton Investment Plus Ann.	800-792-7198	92
Unit. of Omaha Ultrann. Series V	800-453-4933	88
Mass Mutual Panorama	800-234-5606	81
MFS/Sun Life (U.S.) Compass 3	800-752-7215	81
BONDS		
Phoenix Home Life Big Edge Plus	800-843-8348	97
Union Central/Carillon Account	800-825-1551	90
New England Zenith Accumulator	800-777-5897	83
Mass Mutual Flex Extra	800-234-5606	77
Mass Mutual Panorama	800-234-5606	77
INTERNATIONAL STOCK		
Dean Witter Variable Annuity II	800-654-2397	98
WRL Freedom Variable Annuity	800-851-9777	97
Fortis Benefits Opportunity	800-800-2638	94
Templeton Investment Plus Ann.	800-792-7198	93
Ohio National Top B	800-366-6654	91

Note: [1]Score is for category only. **Source:** Morningstar

accounts within the Fidelity Retirement Reserves annuity, and you will pay a 1% annual insurance charge. Buy the same subaccounts through Life of Virginia Commonwealth VA Plus, and you'll face a 1.4% tariff. That difference may seem like a trifle. But investing, say, $25,000 in the Fidelity Retirement Reserves subaccounts rather than Life of Virginia's could net you an extra $11,800 after 20 years.

Don't judge an annuity by its cover. Although many sub-accounts are managed by well-known fund companies and even bear the same names as popular retail funds, don't assume you can count on the same returns in the annuity that shareholders earn in the fund. Even when the manager of an annuity subaccount and its mutual fund counterpart is the same, as is the case with Alger Growth, differences in expenses can lead to varying returns. The Alger Growth mutual fund returned 14.8% annually over three years, while the annuity subaccount gained just 14.3%. Don't dismiss subaccounts whose names are not familiar to you either. Star fund managers run little-known subaccounts. Take the Ohio National annuity's international subaccount, which beat 90% of its peers with a three-year return of 12% annually. It's run by Jean-Marie Eveillard, famed manager of SoGen International fund. To get details on managers and the investment style they plan to use, call the annuity's 800 number and ask for a copy of the prospectus. In addition, Morningstar provides detailed information on more than 3,100 subaccounts for a charge of $5 per subaccount.

◆ ENHANCE YOUR PROFITS ONLINE

More and more investors have discovered the internet is a powerful and profitable investing tool that can open up vast storehouses of timely information. With a few clicks of the mouse, an experienced net navigator can tap into Wall Street research reports on publicly traded companies, view up-to-the-minute stock quotes, gather reams of performance data on thousands of mutual funds, check out the latest rates on CDs and bank loans and even save up to 80% on brokerage commissions by trading securities online.

You can also get bogged down in the sheer number of websites that are now available. Search engines like Yahoo (http://www.yahoo.com) and Lycos (http://www.lycos.com) can narrow these choices down by letting you screen by topic to find websites that interest you. But a search on Yahoo using the subject "invest," for example, yields a still unmanageable list of about 550 sites.

MONEY has identified sites in four areas of personal finance–banking, funds, stocks and brokerage services–whose abundance of practical tips and data can help boost your returns. You can log on to our favorite sites directly by using the internet addresses we supply. Many of them have so-called hypertext links that, once clicked on, will immediately beam you over to other financial sites. You can also find links to sites by logging on to MONEY's website (http://moneymag.com). You will have access to even more sites if you use a popular browser like Netscape Navigator and subscribe to an independent service that links your computer to the net via your home telephone line.

Security problems on the net remain.
It's a considerably safer neighborhood than it used to be, however. Most new browsers including Netscape Navigator and Microsoft Explorer use the latest encryption technology, which encodes your financial information while it is in transit to or from an online bank or brokerage. Online experts say the chances of encrypted data being intercepted and decoded are small. The time for caution comes when you register on a free site or track your portfolio there. Because you hand your information over voluntarily, the site itself has the right to use it as it desires. Many sites merely use that data to customize your account for you. But others might sell it to junk mail marketers. So be wary of what you give away. If you prefer, do what thousands of others have done–register under a pseudonym.

Banking on your net connection.
Given the hype that surrounds computerized banking, you would think the internet is brimming with useful sites for savers and borrowers. It isn't. True, more than a million customers at about 50 institutions bank online. But they do so almost exclusively over direct phone connections between the customers' PCs and the banks' central computers. On the internet proper, banking information is dominated by the banks' home pages, which tend to be sales brochures. Still, a handful of sites can help make you a savvier customer. The most useful is Bank Rate Monitor's Infobank (http://www.bankrate.com), which is operated by the same company that supplies monthly savings yields to MONEY.

Looking for the highest yielding six-month CD? A few clicks of the mouse will pull up a ranking of the six-month CDs offered by 100 banks that market their accounts nationwide. You can't buy CDs from this list over the net. Instead, you call the 800 number listed next to each institution, ask for an application and signature card and then return it with a check by snail mail. Infobank also updates home, credit-card and consumer-loan rates weekly for about 100 cities nationwide. In addition to details on rates and yields, Infobank has a nifty program that lets you calculate loan payments as well. Say you've been tempted by that shiny new 4-by-4 in your auto dealer's showroom. You can forecast the havoc it would wreak on your budget by plugging the details of the loan into the site's payment calculator. A $20,000 car loan at 9% over five years, for example, would put a $415 dent in your monthly cash flow.

Bank of America (http://www.bankamerica.com) lets you transfer money between accounts online and check balances of credit cards or loans you have through the bank. You can pay bills over the net for a $6.50 monthly fee that's waived if your paycheck is directly deposited to the bank. To see whether banks in your area maintain a useful net connection, check out My Bank (http://www.mybank.com), which has a state-by-state listing of bank home pages across the country.

Selecting mutual funds electronically. Fund data once was

so scarce outside stockbrokers' offices that most investors paid hefty sales loads just for the privilege of having a broker recommend a fund. Now virtually every fund group has its own website, and dozens of third-party data sellers offer performance data, screening engines, opinion and analysis. Our favorite site is Networth (http://www.networth.galt.com), a megamall of fund and stock data recently bought by electronic giant Intuit. The site has what we consider the best fund screening engine on the net, allowing you to sort through more than 7,000 funds using as many as 15 different factors ranging from past performance to sales charges to investment minimums. The data comes from Morningstar, the research service that also provides mutual fund data for MONEY.

Once you've whittled down the candidates to a manageable number, Networth lets you investigate each one in more detail. Individual fund reports give you charts of net asset value performance, phone numbers and descriptions of the funds' investment style. Some pages on Networth's site prompt you for a password. But don't worry; any page at the site is free to every registered Networth member. To register, you simply enter your name, address and so forth on an online screen. A close runner-up is Mutual Funds Interactive (http://www.fundsinteractive.com). You can't do screening here. But you can get plenty of free detailed information not available at Networth, including profiles of nearly 50 managers.

You have to pay for most of the information available at Investools (http://www.investools.com), a clearinghouse of research on funds and stocks. But it's worth it. Investools is the only website from which you can download complete Morningstar fund reports ($5 each) as well as fund newsletters. You can often download a prospectus and check out services at a fund company's site. Fidelity (http://www.fid-inv.com) serves up useful tools such as interactive retirement and college planning worksheets plus performance data on funds in the Fidelity Funds Network. Twentieth Century funds (http://www.twentieth-century.com) even lets investors access their accounts and transfer balances from one fund to another over the net.

Logging on to manage your portfolio. There are scores of websites that offer easy access to stock quotes and the latest news on companies and the financial markets. Most sites vying for the attention of serious investors offer plenty of financial data on thousands of individual stocks. Our favorite website for stock research is Stock Smart (http://www.stocksmart.com), which also helps diligent investors compare specific companies with their peers. By clicking on the "Industry Roll-Ups" section of Stock Smart's home page, you can sift through a database of 7,000 companies that is broken down by 27 major industries, ranging from banking to utilities. You also get 100 finer divisions such as savings and loans and water service companies.

Stock Smart has one of the most impressive systems on the net to track the value of your investments. Simply go to the "Your Portfolio" section of the site and enter the names of the stocks, bonds and funds you own, the dates you purchased them, the price per share and commissions you paid. You can then choose to have Stock Smart e-mail you either daily, weekly or monthly updates of the current values of each security and your portfolio overall. The service will also calculate the return you've earned since purchase, although it does not factor in dividend income.

Also worth a visit is Research (http://www.researchmag.com), the home page operated by Research magazine. Although some parts of the site are reserved for professionals, the Investor Net section gives individuals access to a powerful stock-screening feature that can sort some 9,000 stocks by 28 measures, including earnings growth rates and price volatility. Screening is ideal if you're trying to find stocks that jibe with your investing style. For example, with just a few clicks of the mouse, a growth investor can search for companies whose profits are bounding along at, say, 30% a year or better, that have earnings multiples of 20 or less, and that are also rated a buy by Wall Street analysts.

If you're an investor who likes to dig into the minutiae of a company's financial statements, go to the Securities and Exchange Commission's Edgar database (http://www.sec.gov/edgarhp.htm). There you can download at no charge annual and quarterly reports, proxy statements and most other documents that companies are required to file with the SEC. If you're a stock fanatic who likes to keep daily tabs on the issues you own, the Closing Bell site (http://www.merc.com) will e-mail you as often as every day any news on as many as 600 companies that you designate.

Trading your account online. After you've used the net to help you choose your investments, you can save yourself considerable time and cash by buying them there as well. About 15 internet brokerage firms let investors trade stocks, bonds and, in some cases, funds at commissions as much as 80% below what many discount brokers normally charge. One of the best is E Trade (http://www.etrade.com), which charges a flat $15 to buy or sell as many as 5,000 shares of any company that's listed on the New York or American stock exchanges. If you invest in firms whose shares trade over the counter, the tab is a slightly plumper $20. To open an account, you go to E Trade's home page, download an application form (or call 800-786-2575 and ask for one) and mail it back with the $1,000 minimum balance to set up an account. Once the brokerage has received your check, you can begin trading. You simply log on to the site and enter the ticker symbol for the stocks you wish to buy. You can do this any time, day or night, although your orders are executed during the stock market's business hours.

To prevent online thieves and hackers from pilfering your portfolio, you must enter your account password twice–once to get into the E Trade system and a second time to confirm trades. The brokerage also uses Netscape's Secure Commerce server, which employs advanced encryption software to make transactions unreadable by any outsider. Given E Trade's razor-thin commissions, don't expect any personal advice from a broker about what securities you should be buying or selling now. Still, the company does offer some valuable free research options. By clicking onto the Baseline Financial Services link, you can call up historical price and earnings data stretching back as far as five years on some 6,500 companies. You can also read the latest news headlines and stories (as well as retrieve past articles) about specific companies through Reuters and Business Wire, get unlimited free stock quotes and plug recent prices into E Trade's portfolio tracking service.

5

REDUCE

YOUR FUND

PORTFOLIO'S

RISK

*O*ur forecast of a 15% to 20% decline for the stock market should serve as a timely reminder that stock prices do fall as well as rise. That basic fact of life has been easy to forget during this record-breaking bull market that began way back in 1982. In the long run, it's the behavior of the broad market that does most of the work for even the most brilliant investment pro. Money manager Gary Brinson of Brinson Partners in Chicago has painstakingly analyzed the roles that various factors play in determining investment returns. Brinson and a team of researchers found that 92% of investment results can be explained purely by your asset mix. That's the proportions of a portfolio you dedicate to broad investment categories like stocks, bonds and cash. Other factors that many investors view as crucial, such as the choice of specific securities and the timing of purchases and sales, accounted for only 8% of the results.

Say that two investors choose the same asset mix, putting about 60% of their money into stock funds and 40% into bond funds. They will tend to end up with pretty much the same results in the long run, regardless of the particular funds they choose. Meanwhile, an investor with 80% in stock funds and 20% in bond funds will fare differently from the 60–40 investors.

When it comes to investing for retirement, there's a lot to be said for enrolling in the following two-step program. First, buy stock and bond funds with great managers, a consistent investment approach, low volatility, subpar expenses and top after-tax returns. Then hold them as long as is possible. The virtue of this minimalist approach is that your returns compound undisturbed. You also are freed from the temptation to do something every time the market hiccups. Finding portfolios worthy of being cherished for a lifetime isn't easy, of course.

But we've devoted this chapter to several selection processes that are designed to pinpoint a number of funds you can own with confidence.

◆ FAVOR FOUR SURE-FOOTED MAVERICKS

Since investors may be facing soggy weather ahead, now is the time to consider stock funds whose wheels aren't locked into the main market track. Indeed, the four Jeep-like selections profiled below tend to veer in different directions from the large-company U.S. stocks that dominate the S&P 500 index. "Owning such eclectic funds will help reduce the volatility of your portfolio," says former Morningstar strategist John Rekenthaler. "That's because, when blue-chip stocks run into trouble, some of your funds will fall less or even head up."

To find top funds with an independent streak, we first screened Morningstar's database to find those with the lowest correlation to the S&P 500. (In this instance, correlation is a measure of how closely a fund's performance tracks the index.) We translated correlation coefficients into what we dubbed the ISR, or independent streak rating. For example, a fund that always moved in sync with the market would rate an ISR of 0. By contrast, funds with ISRs of 15 or higher tend to unhitch themselves from the overall direction of the S&P.

We then sifted the resulting group of 1,860 unconventional funds to identify those that 1.) ranked in the top third of their investment categories over the past three years and 2.) still had the same manager at the helm. In addition, we looked for funds with subpar risk levels, as measured by Morningstar. This rating measures how often a fund has delivered lower returns than Treasury bills. Generally, a score lower than 1.00 indicates the fund is less risky than the average for its group. We chose the funds with the best combination of consistent returns and high independent streaks in each of four investing categories. They are small company, balanced, real estate and international.

Third Avenue Value. "We buy what other investors hate," says manager Martin Whitman. "That puts us on a different planet from the S&P 500." A classic contrarian, he favors undervalued, little-followed stocks including volatile small companies. Despite his taste for the unconventional, Whitman keeps volatility low by sticking to companies with strong balance sheets. Moreover, those stocks must trade at a price that is

50% below the per-share amount he estimates an outside acquirer would pay for the entire company. This strategy has given the fund a relatively high ISR of 31, as well as a risk level that is 36% less than its peers. Even so, over the past five years, Third Avenue Value has returned a hefty 18% annually, some two percentage points ahead of the S&P. The biggest portion of the portfolio lately was stashed in money management companies including $8.9 billion (assets) Legg Mason. "Being in the money management business is like owning a toll booth on the George Washington bridge," says Whitman. "You just sit back and collect the cash." His second-largest stake was smaller semiconductor equipment manufacturers.

UAM FPA Crescent. At first glance, this fund looks like your basic balanced portfolio. But a closer look shows it to be a winning but oddball blend of small and midsized company stocks and junk bonds, which have contributed to its lofty ISR of 68. Even so, the three-year-old fund is far less risky than you might think. Its Morningstar risk score is 61% less than the typical fund in its category. Manager Steve Romick hews to a value approach by looking for companies that are expanding earnings by at least 10% annually yet trade at a 30% discount to the price they would fetch if an acquirer bought the whole company. "By investing in growing stocks at a discount, I can meet my goal of delivering topnotch returns with less risk," says Romick. He lately has been finding values in the retail sector, including $1.4 billion (annual sales) arts-and-crafts supplier Michael's Stores and $156 million International House of Pancakes. For the fixed-income portion of his portfolio, he scoops up lower-quality bonds issued by companies with proven ability to pay their debts. These bargain-hunting strategies have helped Romick log an impressive return of 18% annually, which places the balanced fund in the top tier of its investment category.

Cohen & Steers Realty Shares. For co-managers Martin Cohen and Robert Steers, REITs (real estate investment trusts) are the only real way to invest in real estate. "Our stocks must be pure, property-owning real estate plays," says Cohen. "Unlike some of our competitors, we won't buy related stocks like building companies." Because of their strict criteria, this fund sports a towering ISR of 99. To find rewarding real estate stocks, the managers first identify regions of the country with strong economic growth and healthy real estate markets. Then they screen those locales for companies that have cheap prices, above-average yields and solid management. More than 50% of the portfolio recently was invested in office buildings and regional malls. "In many places, there have been few new offices built since the early 1950s," says Cohen. "So occupancy rates will stay strong for years." Large holdings include $1.5 billion Spieker Properties, an owner of industrial properties on the West Coast, and $2 billion shopping center operator Vornado Realty Trust, which recently purchased several properties in New York City. With such picks, Cohen & Steers Realty has earned a sterling five-year return of 19% annually, beating the S&P 500. And that gain was produced with 17% less risk than its peers.

SoGen Overseas. Few investors have more experience spotting values off the beaten track than veteran fund manager Jean-Marie Eveillard. The French-born Eveillard has run top-ranked SoGen International, a global fund, for 18 years. And in 1993 he launched SoGen Overseas to focus exclusively on smaller foreign stocks. "The foreign markets for small companies are much less efficient than in the U.S., which provides us with great opportunities," says Eveillard. Unlike many value investors, Eveillard does not rely on a rigid stock-picking formula. "Some value investors will only buy if the price is truly cheap, even if the business is only fair, while others will buy a good business, even if the price isn't that cheap," notes Eveillard. "We own a combination of both." At last count about half of the fund's stockholdings were invested in the developed markets of Europe, with another 12% in Japan and 15% spread among developing markets such as Hong Kong and New Zealand. A typical holding is $1.9 billion Buderus, a German maker of residential heating systems. "Although the German economy is flat on its back, Buderus is extremely profitable by that country's standards," Eveillard says. It's little wonder that SoGen Overseas posts a solid ISR of 59. Even so, over the past three years, the fund has returned nearly 11% annually to rank in the top 14% of its peers. And the fund has delivered those returns with 66% less volatility than other foreign stock funds.

◆ BUY AND FORGET THESE SOLID FUNDS

Want to buy a stock fund or two that are worth holding forever? To identify such exemplars, we began by screening Morningstar's database for funds that have superior returns over at least 10 years. That means the funds lived through both October 1987, when the worst crash since 1929 knocked 23% off the market's value in a single day, and 1990, when stock funds lost 7% as a group for the year. We did make one exception, however. We settled for a stellar five-year record for small-company funds. Top contenders that have been around for a decade are either closed to new investors or too large, in our view, to manage small stocks efficiently. In addition, we required our final selections to have earned their returns while taking less risk than their peers.

All those strictures narrowed the field to just over 100 funds, which we cut to our finalists by subjecting them to the following criteria. The same manager or investment team must have been in place for the entire 10-year period and show every sign of staying put. This ensures that the pros you hire today are the ones responsible for the fund's great record—and are the same ones you'll have managing your money tomorrow. We also looked for annual expenses below the 1.4% norm for U.S. stock funds and 1.9% for foreign funds. The less a fund clips you in fees, the more you keep for your nest egg. And annual turnover could not exceed 35%, vs. 85% for stock funds overall. Turnover is the measure of how often the fund trades its stocks. A turnover rate of 35% means about a third of a portfolio's holdings are sold that year.

Whether you buy one or all of the no-load funds profiled below, you can be assured that they have topped their peers at providing impressive gains at below-average risk.

Longleaf Partners Small Cap. Unlike many of its small-company competitors, this fund isn't laden with snazzy technology stocks. Instead, Longleaf focuses on down-to-earth small stocks in businesses like real estate, life insurance and basic manufacturing. Memphis-based managers Mason Hawkins and Staley Cates use their contacts among company managements to locate topnotch small firms that aren't widely covered by Wall Street analysts. When they find them, they dissect the financial statements to narrow the search to those trading at no more than 60% of their liquidation value, or cash flow after capital expenditures.

Take Longleaf holding White River, a $124 million holding company. Among White River's many mundane businesses is providing software and estimating services for auto insurance and car repair firms. Hawkins and Cates figure that the company's assets, including cash and a securities portfolio, are worth $90 per share. Yet the stock trades for just $63.

Says Hawkins: "It doesn't take a clairvoyant to see that buying a company trading this far below its true value removes a lot of risk and provides room for ample gains." Over the past three years the fund has returned 17% annually, vs. 10% for the Russell 2000 small-stock index. And it has done so with 27% less risk than small-cap value funds as a group. Says Hawkins: "There are lots of great small companies out there. But not everyone has the patience and discipline to find them."

Strong Schafer Value. Don't bother asking manager David Schafer to forecast Federal Reserve policy or interest rates. "I wouldn't bet a nickel on my guess of where the economy will be a year from now," he says. "But fortunately I've learned how to judge value in individual stocks." The midsized and large companies owned by his fund have PEs below the market's 17 and projected growth rates above the 7% forecast for S&P 500 stocks. If an issue doesn't meet either of these criteria, Schafer won't consider it. This approach has led him to overlooked stocks in mundane industries. Consider $4.4 billion Owens-Illinois, which makes beer bottles and other glass containers. The PE based on this year's estimated earnings is a lowly 14. Yet the Toledo company has an earnings growth rate of more than 10% annually. "This is no high flyer," says Schafer with considerable understatement, "just a solid company increasing earnings year after year." Schafer's well-schooled eye for values has resulted in a five-year return of 18% annually with 26% less risk than the norm.

Babson Value. Manager Nick Whitridge screens a computer database for some 1,250 large companies, looking for cheap thrills. These are stocks that have below-market PEs and above-average yields. But instead of stopping there, as many value managers do, Whitridge scours the ranks of companies with beat-up shares to find those that are increasing their earnings for the current quarter vs. the last quarter and the past 12 months. "The classic mistake value investors make is buying stocks too early and then watching them languish," he explains. "By looking hard at current growth rates along with basic valuation, I can spot shares that are close to emerging from Wall Street's doghouse."

Once Whitridge sinks his teeth into such a stock, he holds on like a terrier. Last year his portfolio had 11% turnover, a rate more typical of an index fund. He increased his stake in Kmart, the $34.7 billion discount retailer, in 1995 when the stock was selling at $6 and virtually every Chicken Little on Wall Street said the company was about to go bankrupt. Today Kmart shares trade around $13. Says Whitridge: "When investors overreact to a company's temporary setbacks, there's often an opportunity for long-term gains." Indeed, over the past five years, Babson Value has returned almost 17% annually, vs. 15% for the S&P 500. Better yet, according to Morningstar, the fund has posted those gains while taking 31% less risk than stock funds overall.

Vanguard Windsor II.

Vanguard Windsor II. This large-cap fund's tiny 0.4% expenses are half the 0.8% average for all our selections. That gives the fund's lead manager, Jim Barrow, nearly a half-percentage point advantage over his peers in the annual performance derby. His strict buy discipline also helps. Barrow looks for companies trading at least 20% below the S&P 500's PE and yielding 40% more than the market's payout. That's how he got to $76 billion Philip Morris, whose shares retreated earlier this year as investors reacted (or overreacted in Barrow's view) to the tobacco industry's potential legal problems. The company, which has boosted its earnings roughly 18% annually for 35 years, recently yielded a lush 4% and trades at a PE of 16. Says Dallas-based Barrow: "This is a powerhouse company whose profits have grown like a weed despite the legal cloud." Once he buys, Barrow hangs on. The fund has an average turnover of 25%. "I don't worry about what kind of backflip the market is doing today," he says. "Over time, good, cheap stocks rise in value." And so has Windsor II, returning 16% annually over the past five years while taking 28% less risk than the norm.

Vanguard International Growth.

Vanguard International Growth. This globetrotter concentrates on blue chips in 24 countries. London-based manager Richard Foulkes, in charge since the fund started in 1981, buys steadily growing global market leaders with strong balance sheets and proven management. Foulkes, who keeps his fund's turnover below 30%, doesn't sweat the day-to-day price fluctuations in his stocks. "Even if I buy at the wrong moment," he says, "I can still make good profits over three years or more." These days, Foulkes is fond of Japan, where PEs have dropped dramatically from a historic average of more than 100 to a mere 40, making for rare bargains in world-leading companies. One favorite is $11 billion Fuji Photo, a global brand-name leader that's the No. 2 film maker after Kodak. Yet Fuji's stock recently traded for 23 times estimated 1997 earnings, a 40% discount to the typical Japanese stock. Helped by low expenses of 0.6%, vs. 1.9% for his peers, Foulkes has proven himself quite worldly when it comes to fattening his shareholders' wallets. The fund has returned nearly 17% annually over the past 15 years, handily beating Morgan Stanley's benchmark EAFE index of foreign stocks.

◆ HIRE YOUR OWN MONEY MANAGER

If you've ever fantasized about having your retirement money looked after by the same exclusive investment advisers who cater to the rich, your dream has come true. In the past three years, more than 50 firms that invest for well-heeled individuals, pension funds and large corporations have launched mutual funds. We've analyzed five outstanding examples of these funds, each a no-load portfolio that lets you invest like a bigshot even if you have only $1,000 to $10,000 to begin. Buying these funds doesn't assure you of market-whipping profits. But a couple of factors increase the odds that institutional managers will succeed. First, their clients demand that they follow a highly disciplined investing strategy. That means these managers are less likely to chase the hot stock of the day and then get burned in a flameout. And there's less pressure to bulk up fund assets to generate management fees because the bulk of these firms' revenues come from their private customers. Thus these funds can maneuver around the markets like efficient speedboats rather than cumbersome oil tankers.

We began our hunt for these funds with the help of Performance Analytics, a Chicago firm that tracks 3,000 institutional accounts. To identify outfits with the best records, we asked Performance Analytics to screen for 120 top performers from a range of investment styles, based on recent five-year returns. We then searched that elite group for firms that sponsor mutual funds managed in the same style as the private accounts with minimum initial investments of $10,000 or less. We weren't looking only for big returns. We also sought accounts that held up well in down markets. As you'll see, the last three funds discussed below lack long-term track records. But given the impressive pedigrees of the firms that spawned them, experts believe these portfolios will prove themselves to be winners in the years ahead.

Westwood Equity and Westwood Balanced. These two funds (minimum initial investment $1,000; 800-937-8966) are our only selections that have been around long enough to establish themselves as reliable overachievers. Launched in 1987, Westwood Equity has earned a five-year return of 18% annually, outpacing the average stock fund by 4.6 percentage points while taking 30% less risk. Similarly, Westwood Balanced, founded in 1991, has returned 15% during the past five years, vs. 11% for balanced funds overall. Says manager Susan Byrne: "Our style is to capture gains in a fabulous market and avoid the carnage in a horrible one."

Byrne employs the same investing approach at the funds as she does at Westwood Management, the Dallas-based firm that invests $1.1 billion for pension funds and college endowments. She and her team of seven analysts evaluate the prospects for the U.S. economy for the coming 12 months, then pick the securities they think will excel in that climate. Says Peggy McKean, a managing director with consultant Stolper & Co.: "Susan Byrne is unmatched in her ability to identify market trends and pick the best stocks to capitalize on them." For the year ahead, Byrne foresees 2.5% inflation and sluggish 8% growth in corporate profits. Thus she expects bonds to outgain stocks, 7% vs. 5%. So she has boosted her bondholdings in Westwood Balanced to 40% from 32% a year ago, dividing most of that stake between Treasury securities and high-quality corporate bonds maturing in two to 10 years. For Westwood Equity's stock portfolio, Byrne has been scooping up high-dividend stocks such as $23.5 billion GTE, which she thinks can more than double the overall market's gain.

Montag & Caldwell Growth. Big clients like Wake Forest University fork over a minimum of $20 million to tap into the investing skills of Ron Canakaris and the 10 other managers at Montag & Caldwell, the venerable $8.4 billion Atlanta investment firm. But you can buy the firm's services for just $2,500 via the $326 million Montag & Caldwell Growth fund (800-992-8151) launched in November 1994. Canakaris and company scout for the stocks of large growth companies that they calculate are selling for at least 15% to 20% less than the value of the their future earnings. That approach has driven the firm's stock accounts to return about 20% annually over the past five years. Canakaris lately has been loading up his portfolio with shares of large, undervalued U.S. technology and consumer-goods companies that do a sizable portion of their business overseas. He figures such companies stand to profit from robust growth abroad if the U.S. economy slows.

Canakaris' private accounts have weathered market squalls well. In the past five years, these accounts were 91% less risky than the S&P 500 in quarters when the index declined, according to Performance Analytics. "Our clients don't like rollercoaster rides," says Canakaris. "So we aim for consistent returns."

CRM Small Cap Value. Cramer Rosenthal McGlynn is a $2.5 billion New York City investment adviser that focuses on rapidly growing small companies with total market values of $1 billion or less. And the tony clients who have shelled out $5 million or more to invest with CRM have reason to be pleased. Over the past five years, the firm's small-cap private accounts have returned 19% annually, vs. 16% for the Russell 2000 index of small companies. Since October 1995, individual investors with $10,000 or more to invest have been able to cash in on this firm's small-company expertise by buying into CRM Small Cap Value (800-844-8258).

Managers Ronald McGlynn and Jay Abramson use their contacts among investment bankers, company executives and even their own high-net-worth clients to find undiscovered small-cap gems that are on the verge of a major change, such as a merger or joint venture, that can boost their stock price by 50% or more within two years. Still, CRM's small-company accounts have been 38% less risky than the Russell 2000 in falling markets. One thing that contributes to that outstanding performance is the firm's insistence on buying stocks selling for substantially less than the companies' intrinsic worth. One notable pick from the portfolio is $1.2 billion Mascotech, which forges engine parts for General Motors, Ford and other auto companies. Mascotech's profit margins are a racy 13%, vs. 5% to 9% for its peers. Yet the stock's PE of 10 is 15% to 25% below those of its competitors.

UAM Jacobs International Octagon. This portfolio ($2,000 minimum; 800-638-7983) opened to investors only in January. And the boutique that launched it, $80 million Jacobs Asset Management, dates back only to 1995. Not to worry. Fund manager Dan Jacobs spent 10 years at international powerhouse Templeton Investments, where he managed $2 billion for corporate pension and private accounts and ran the $1.4 billion Templeton Smaller Companies Growth fund. During the past five years, Jacobs' institutional accounts have gained 19% annually. That was more than double the 8.5% return for the EAFE index of foreign stocks in the developed markets of Europe, Australasia and the Far East. Even more impressive, Jacobs' private accounts actually gained when the EAFE index fell. In choosing stocks for his fund, Jacobs emulates investing legend John Templeton, scouring the globe for stocks whose prices have been beaten down but appear on the verge of a turnaround. Jacobs lately has found the most alluring bargains in Europe (36% of assets) and emerging markets (33%), such as Mexico and Brazil. One favorite recent buy is $1 billion supermarket chain Bompreco in Brazil. The company's shares trade at a depressed PE of 10. But Jacobs predicts profit growth of 15% to 20% annually for the next five years.

◆ BOND FUNDS WILL EARN MORE RESPECT

They seem to have earned a bad name with investors lately. Back in 1993, investors crammed $114 billion into fixed-income funds, nearly as much as they packed into stock funds. Many of those bond fund investors apparently believed they were merely buying higher-yielding versions of bank accounts. Then in 1994 they found out the difference between guaranteed bank yields and gyrating bond returns. As interest rates rose throughout the year, bond prices fell, and U.S. taxable bond funds lost 3% as a group. The flood of cash promptly dried up. In 1995 and 1996, investors have added a relatively meager $4.6 billion to bond funds while pouring an astonishing $307 billion into stock funds.

Ignoring bonds is a mistake, however. First, they tend to zig when stocks sag. Since 1926, there have been eight calendar years in which U.S. stocks fell at least 10%. (The average decline was 22%.) But in only one of those years, 1931, did intermediate government bonds lose money. By contrast, stocks tumbled 43% that year. In the long run, bonds also earn their returns more predictably than stocks do. Let's say you buy a 10-year Treasury note at its par value of $10,000, with a 6.5% interest coupon. Simply hang on and you're certain to get your $10,000 back in 2007. Every six months from now till then this bond will pay you $325, for a total of $6,500. Along the way, you'll be able to reinvest the interest. Assuming an average rate of 6.5% when you reinvest, you'll earn another $2,458 as your interest compounds.

Well-managed bond funds enjoy the same predictability over the long term. True, bond funds never mature the way bonds do. So you can't simply hold on and be sure of getting your full principal back. Bond fund shares gain or lose value as interest rates rise and fall. But good bond fund managers concentrate on keeping net asset value as stable as possible and avoid using risky strategies to pump up yield. At these funds, price changes have tended to cancel each other out over periods of 10 years or more, leaving you with a total return roughly equal to the interest rate the fund was paying at the time you invested.

What's more, bonds may actually return more, not less, than stocks in coming years. Here's why. Stock returns are driven by dividend yield, growth in earnings and changes in market valuation. The current dividend yield on stocks is 2%. We can't be certain how fast corporate earnings will grow, although the long-term average is a bit more than 6%. Add that to the dividend yield, and you get a projected average return on stocks of about 8% annually. Market valuation, which is the price investors are willing to pay for each dollar of earnings, is pure guesswork. All we know for sure is that investors recently were paying as much as $20 for each $1 of the previous 12 months' earnings, vs. the long-term average PE multiple of 15.

If that already lofty earnings multiple climbs even higher, stocks could return more than 8% annually during the next few years. If it stays the same, stocks will earn about 8%. If it sinks, stocks will earn less. For example, if the earnings multiple reverts to its long-term average of 15, stocks will return somewhere between 6% and 7% annually for the next decade. If it dips even lower, as it often has in the past, stocks could return even less. Thus it's not just possible, but quite likely, that stocks will do no better than bonds during the next 10 years.

The main difference between the two types of investments is that you can get a more reliable return of 6% to 7% on bonds. With stocks, you might do better than that and you might do worse. In short, you should always own a sizable slug of stocks, no matter what your risk tolerance, because they offer the hope of superior returns over the long haul. But you should always own some bonds because they offer the virtue of more predictable returns.

When investing in bonds, it's also important to keep taxes in mind. Because bond funds throw off a lot of taxable income, you want to hold them in a tax-deferred savings account, such as an IRA or 401(k) plan, if that's possible. Or you can invest instead in municipal bond funds, which generate tax-free income and normally produce higher after-tax yields for taxpayers in all but the lowest federal tax bracket.

Why Vanguard excels at bond funds. Ian MacKinnon, who supervises fixed-income investments at fund giant Vanguard, typically keeps 80% of his own personal portfolio in stocks and 20% in bonds. But recently, MacKinnon cut back to a 65-35 mix of stocks and bonds. He thinks that level is a pretty good one for a moderate risk investor. If you think you crave higher risk, an 80-20 mix may still be your speed. If you are on the conservative side, fifty–fifty or even 40% stocks, 60% bonds may be right. In any case, there's no better place to shop for bond funds than MacKinnon's Vanguard. The firm's rock-bottom costs give its funds a built-in advantage. The typical junk bond fund, for instance, charges 1.4% of assets in annual expenses. The typical Treasury bond fund charges 0.8%. Vanguard's junk fund charges 0.3%, as does its intermediate Treasury fund.

Vanguard's bond funds also tend to outperform their competitors by considerably more than their expense advantage alone. MacKinnon and other Vanguard managers invest for total return, not maximum yield. This approach gives their funds more stable and predictable results than their rivals. In addition, Vanguard's managers have a good record of cautiously shortening maturities when they think interest rates may rise and lengthening them moderately when they think rates will fall.

In a tax-sheltered retirement account, we recommend that you buy an investment-grade fund such as **Vanguard Intermediate–Term Bond Index**. It has returned 7.2% over the past 12 months and 7.8% annually over the past three years. Also consider combining higher-returning **Vanguard GNMA** (8.5% over the past 12 months; 8.5% annually over three years) with a junk bond portfolio like **Vanguard High–Yield Corporate** (12.8% over 12 months; 11.7% annually over three years). MacKinnon feels that junk bonds offer more than enough yield to compensate for their higher risk.

You can take bond diversification one step further with funds that hold debt securities of all kinds from around the globe in a kind of fixed-income goulash. Three such funds to consider for their moderate expenses, eclectic diversification and astute management are **Harbor Bond, Janus Flexible Income** and **Loomis Sayles Bond**. In your taxable accounts, you could blend **Vanguard Intermediate–Term U.S. Treasury**, which is exempt from most state income taxes; and **Vanguard Municipal Bond Intermediate–Term**. It's a so-called national muni fund that invests broadly in bonds from around the nation and is exempt from federal and some state income tax.

6

GROW AND
GUARD YOUR
401(K) MONEY

*E*ven though nearly 80% of eligible Americans are savvy enough to invest in their company 401(k) retirement plans, most employees aren't revving up the account to its full savings potential. One of four 401(k) participants contributes less than 4% of his or her income rather than the 6% maximum most plans allow. Half of all contributors ages 31 to 45 say they take a conservative approach to investing a 401(k). One of five employees who own 401(k) accounts borrows from them.

These are financial blunders you can't afford to make. Americans increasingly are on their own when it comes to financing their golden years. Social Security faces an uncertain future. Traditional employer-paid pensions usually require decades-long careers at one company–an anachronism today. A typical worker's retirement now stretches to 20 or even 30 years, compared with 10 not so long ago. Therefore, a hefty 401(k) account could be the difference between retiring comfortably or moving into your kid's converted garage while working part-time.

The rules for 401(k) investing are start young, take risks early and leave the money alone. Stash as much of your income as you can and put that money in growth-oriented investments that figure to earn 7% to 9% annually. To help get your account compounding on the right track, check out the strategies and advice described in this final chapter devoted solely to your crucial 401(k).

◆ MASTER THE BASICS OF YOUR PLAN

If you aren't now eligible to join a 401(k), you probably will be some-time soon. Fully 95% of American companies with more than 5,000 employees offer a 401(k), whose name comes from the section of the tax code that authorized it. By 2001 nearly 30 million workers will be able to join one, according to estimates by Access Research, a benefits consultant based in Windsor, Conn. If you work for a nonprofit group or in the public sector, you likely will have access to similar savings plans called 403(b) or 457 accounts.

Three factors combine to make 401(k)s an unbeatable investment. Each dollar you tuck into your account is deducted from your taxable income. So you avoid federal and state taxes (except in Pennsylvania) on that money until you withdraw it. Someone in the 28% federal tax bracket who puts $2,400 into a 401(k) each year saves a quick $672 in federal taxes. What's more, all the interest, dividends and capital gains that you earn in your account continue to grow tax free (again, until withdrawal). And for good measure, nine out of 10 companies that offer 401(k)s sweeten the pot with money of their own. The corporate treasury typically will add 50¢ to every dollar you put in (capping its contribution at 3% of your salary). Some large companies offer a dollar-for-dollar match.

Most workers who are eligible for 401(k)s do participate in them. If you're among those who don't, perhaps you think you can do better investing on your own outside the plan. But you are overlooking the awesome advantage of deferring taxes. Say a 35–year–old saves 6% of a $60,000 salary in a taxable portfolio of funds. If that money earns 8% a year, he would have roughly $284,000 by age 65, assuming a 28% federal tax rate. If he were to invest that money in a 401(k), he eventually would end up with $571,700. That's more than twice as much. He would have to pay regular income taxes on the money he withdraws. But he would be able to take the money out gradually, lessening the tax bite, and leave the rest to continue growing tax deferred. Even if he rashly withdrew it all at once, he would be left with $366,000 after taxes. That's 29% more than he would have accumulated in a taxable investment.

There's a catch to 401(k)s, of course. It's totally up to you to make these plans work. You have to pony up the savings dollars, and you must make all the investment decisions. Save too little or pick the wrong investments, and your retirement may be considerably less comfortable. You may be wary of joining a 401(k) because you're reluctant to lock up your money for such a long time. True, short of becoming disabled, you generally can't get your money back before age 59.5

without owing a 10% penalty on the amount you withdraw plus regular income taxes. Most companies, however, let you borrow against your account without penalty or tax as long as you pay the loan back. Most also let you permanently withdraw money for so-called hardship expenses, though you will still face taxes and the 10% penalty. (For our advice, see "Withdrawing Money in Retirement" later in this chapter.)

Moreover, if you leave the company, you can take your money with you, rolling it over into an IRA or possibly your new company's retirement plan. That way you can avoid paying penalties and taxes. Depending on how long you've been in the plan, you'll be able to take some or all of your company's matching contributions as well. In a process known as vesting, you are entitled to a greater share of your company's matching funds the longer you stay in the plan. Schedules vary from company to company. But federal law usually requires full vesting after no more than seven years. Your benefits counselor can tell you how soon you can sign up. At most companies, you first have to be on the payroll for a year.

Why you should invest to the max. You may think you have to wait until you're bringing home a big paycheck to start building your 401(k). Not so. Even for someone earning an entry-level salary, the key is to start early. Say that you are 25 years old with a job that pays $25,000 a year. If you save 6% of your salary, or just $125 a month, get a 50% match and earn 8% on that money, you would end up with $1.1 million by age 65. (That's assuming you get steady annual wage hikes.) And scraping together even a few dollars more can give you a surprisingly big payoff. If you're capable of putting away 8% of your pay, your account would balloon to $1.4 million by your 65th birthday.

You typically can set aside 15% of your salary up to the IRS maximum of around $9,500 a year. That amount is increased periodically for inflation. But some employers cap your contributions at 10% of salary or less mainly to comply with complex IRS regulations aimed at making sure plans don't disproportionately benefit a company's best-paid employees. Even if you can't afford to part with 10% or 15% of your paycheck, try to come up with enough to qualify for your employer's top matching contribution. You usually can invest your employer's money in the same way you deploy yours, though some employers require you to keep their share in the company's stock. About 20% of employers also allow workers to make after-tax contributions. That means you pay normal income taxes on the money before it goes into your account. Although companies rarely match after-tax contributions, they can be a handy way to boost your savings. And you're generally free to withdraw them at any time without paying a penalty.

Exercise your plan's investment options. Once you figure out how much to save, your next step is to decide where to put the money. Chances are you will have plenty of choices thanks mainly to Labor Department guidelines that encourage companies to provide a broad range of investment options. The typical 401(k) offers six mutual funds, compared with only three or four five years ago. The mix might consist of a money-market fund, a "stable value" account or bond fund, a balanced fund, a growth fund, an aggressive growth or small-company fund, and an international fund. Some large corporations give you access to 35 or more funds. The funds that are available can be either retail funds (the kind open to all investors) or private accounts managed by banks, insurance companies and money-management firms. The retail funds are becoming more common because fund companies are bidding aggressively to capture 401(k) business. Employers also like the idea of being able to provide brand name funds that their employees may recognize. The advantage of retail funds is that, by law, they must provide investors with extensive information including a detailed prospectus that describes the fund's expenses. Most private funds are not required to disclose that much detail about their operations.

Track the progress of your account. By law your employer is required to give you an account statement only once a year if you request one. Most plan sponsors provide quarterly reports. And 58% let you get information on your account, including its current value and the latest performance of your funds, via a toll-free 800 number. Many large plans also allow you to change your investment choices or move money from one fund to the other whenever you like. While that flexibility is a nice perk, don't get carried away with it. Remember that your 401(k) is a long-term investment. There's no need to be constantly fine-tuning your portfolio. For more on how to manage your 401(k), see "Perfect Your Plan's Investment Mix" on page 161.

There is no law requiring that all plan expenses be disclosed to the participant. Moreover, financial services companies often make pricing complicated by, say, levying different charges depending on the number or type of transactions that plan participants actually make. Even the people in charge of your plan may be in the dark. A survey by Dalbar Associates, a Boston market research firm, found that 78% of plan sponsors did not know the investment management expenses of their 401(k) plans. Most of those expenses are investment management fees that come out of your account, reducing your earnings. While most companies will pick up the administrative costs, some tap employee accounts for those fees as well.

So what is a reasonable amount to pay? In general, you should pay no more than 1% in total costs. Keeping your costs that low can be difficult if your 401(k) offers retail funds, however. That's because you may be paying management fees that are twice those of other accounts. For example, expense ratios for retail U.S. stock funds average about 1.4%, compared with 0.5% for a comparable institutional fund. Fund companies are piling up profits on their 401(k) business by levying a retail expense structure on institutional accounts, where the costs are significantly lower.

◆ BEWARE OF GOLD-PLATED EXPENSES

The drawbacks of many 401(k)s are huge hidden costs. Right now some 24 million workers are counting on the savings they have stashed in their plans for their future financial security. In only four years, these burgeoning accounts will nearly double to $1.5 trillion, enough to provide pensions for 18% of the labor force. Yet consider these disturbing facts.

Many hefty fees may be hidden. If all 401(k)s held their fees to the level charged by moderately priced mutual funds or investment managers, workers would save approximately $1.5 billion a year. The excess fees take major bites out of employee savings because most 401(k) participants are investing in their plan for a decade or more. A typical 35-year-old employee who participated in a high-cost plan for 30 years would retire with 25% less than he would have collected under a low-cost plan. In all, that's a $244,000 shortfall.

Few employees know they pay any 401(k) fees, let alone how much they are. Most plans don't regularly disclose the costs in their quarterly account statements, as every mutual fund is required in its prospectus. One reason is antiquated laws like ERISA (the Employee Retirement

Income Security Act) governing retirement plans. It was written in 1974, six years before the first 401(k) plan was drafted. ERISA was designed for pensions that are managed exclusively by professional investors. But employees make investment decisions in their 401(k). "Employees are increasingly told that retirement is their responsibility," says Ted Benna, the pension consultant who invented the 401(k) plan. "Yet they are not given significant information they need to do the job."

Employers often fail as fiduciaries. That means they must act responsibly to protect the workers enrolled in the savings plans. Among those fiduciary duties is to make sure that the fees 401(k) participants pay are reasonable. Yet few employers do. Many bosses at companies with small or midsize plans are scarcely more informed about 401(k) costs than are their workers. Worse, those who do focus on expenses increasingly are more intent on shifting them onto the employees than on reducing them. Only 37% of employers surveyed in a 1995 study said they still paid the full administrative cost of 401(k)s, compared with 48% the previous year. Warns David Wray of the Profit-Sharing/401(k) Council of America: "High-cost 401(k)s are a lawsuit waiting to happen."

Before you go running to the courthouse, there are steps you can take to protect your savings. First, employees should educate themselves about their 401(k) costs and then pressure their employers to minimize fees. Determined employees may soon discover they have more power than they imagine. Time and again, the highly competitive 401(k) industry has responded rapidly to investor demands. For example, the typical plan now offers six investment options, vs. four just five years ago, as well as such amenities as a toll-free help line, an investment newsletter and simplified loan processing. Consultant Benna says that if consumers insisted on more competitive prices, the industry would have to comply. The outside firms hired to run the plan are typically an arm of a fund family, bank, insurer or benefits consulting firm. These so-called plan providers often charge high fees for their administrative and investment management services. Here is a closer look at exactly how you are getting overcharged:

Fees rarely are justified by services. Your 401(k) administrative fees cover such services as keeping records, mailing quarterly statements, staffing toll-free lines, complying with government regulations and so on. The plan provider typically bills the employer for these. The charges may vary from a low flat fee of $1,000 for a small plan to $200,000 or more for a large plan. The provider often tacks on a separate charge of about $25 per participant. The far larger part of 401(k) costs is the provider's investment fees. As with mutual fund management fees, the money-management firm (which may also be the provider/administrator) collects these fees in return for selecting and monitoring the plan's investments. The charges are calculated as a percentage of the plan's assets and deducted directly from those assets. In other words, you pay them but don't feel the hand in your pocket.

Economics 101 says your 401(k)'s costs should depend on your plan's size and the service you get. But these costs can be as irrational as airline ticket pricing. For example, a nationwide survey of 401(k) providers by the Baltimore-based pension research firm HR Investment Consultants found that total per capita costs for a 100-participant plan with $3 million in assets ranged from a low of $219 to a high of $861. That's a difference of almost 300%. For a 1,000-employee plan with $30 million in assets, there was an even wider spread of $141 to $755, or more than 425%.

Similar results were found in a survey conducted by consultant Steve Butler of Pension Dynamics in Lafayette, Calif. Butler asked 40 leading 401(k) providers to bid on a large-company plan with 4,000 enrolled workers and a small-company program with 100 participants. The 25 fee quotes he received showed minor differences in the services promised but wide discrepancies in price. The total quoted prices for the plans' first year ranged from $23 to $55 per participant for the large-company plan and from $54 to $383 for the small one. (Refer to the table "How Fees Differ Among 401(k) Plans" opposite.) The most expensive provider in Butler's survey, insurer Cigna, proposed to charge participants in the small-company plan more than seven times as much as fund behemoth Vanguard, the most efficient 401(k) manager he polled. Butler says the steep price some providers charge may have more to do with greed than with their level of service. "In many cases, you are not getting extra value by paying a high price for your 401(k)," he says.

Smaller companies can really get fleeced. As our table shows, employees in small-company plans can pay five times more on average in the first year than workers at big firms. That's partly because

◆ How Fees Differ Among 401(k) Plans

To find out how much 401(k) costs may vary for similar plans, MONEY asked benefits consultant Steve Butler to collect fee quotes for an actual large company and a small firm from service providers. Butler received 25 responses that are listed below.

LARGE PLAN; 4,000 PARTICIPANTS; $20 MILLION IN ASSETS

PROVIDER	TOTAL ANNUAL PLAN COST	TOTAL ADMINISTRATIVE COST[2]	WHAT YOU PAY TOTAL INVESTMENT COST[3]	FIRST-YEAR COST FOR YOU	YOUR TOTAL EXPENSES OVER FIVE YEARS[4]
Fleet Investment	$275,600	$54,600	$221,000	$55.25	$1,984
Invesco	300,000	113,000	187,000	46.75	1,709
Mass Mutual	221,500	48,000	173,500	43.38	1,593
American Century	248,500	80,500	168,000	42.00	1,547
Prudential	201,750	41,500	160,250	40.01	1,491
Fidelity Direct	357,850	208,100	149,750	37.44	1,403
American Funds	186,890	52,640	134,250	33.56	1,205
Principal Financial[1]	269,345	176,345	93,000	23.25	914

SMALL PLAN; 100 PARTICIPANTS; $2 MILLION IN ASSETS

PROVIDER	TOTAL ANNUAL PLAN COST	TOTAL ADMINISTRATIVE COST[2]	WHAT YOU PAY TOTAL INVESTMENT COST[3]	FIRST-YEAR COST FOR YOU	YOUR TOTAL EXPENSES OVER FIVE YEARS[4]
Cigna	$42,775	$4,500	$38,275	$382.75	$3,301
American Express	37,825	4,350	33,475	334.75	2,922
Merrill Lynch	34,575	3,900	30,675	306.75	2,688
Aetna	35,100	4,500	30,600	306.00	2,750
Mass Mutual	30,250	4,900	25,350	253.50	2,314
Fidelity Advisor	32,250	8,500	23,750	237.50	2,130
Fleet Investment	25,600	3,500	22,100	221.00	1,984
Putnam	22,225	2,975	19,250	192.50	1,754
Invesco	26,900	8,200	18,700	187.00	1,709
American Century	21,900	5,100	16,800	168.00	1,547
Prudential	19,525	3,500	16,025	160.25	1,491
T. Rowe Price	20,400	5,100	15,300	153.00	1,417
Fidelity Direct	24,825	9,850	14,975	149.75	1,403
Franklin Templeton	17,003	2,350	14,653	146.53	1,372
American Funds	16,625	3,200	13,425	134.25	1,205
Principal Financial[1]	30,246	20,946	9,300	93.00	825
Vanguard	11,375	6,000	5,375	53.75	585

Notes: [1]For plan using nonproprietary mutual funds only [2]Includes annual base recordkeeping fee, per-participant charges and trustee fees [3]Includes asset-based expenses and weighted average fund expense ratio that's based on equal investments in the provider's top-performing funds for each asset class, excluding money funds [4]Based on average annual expenses, $10,000 contributed annually to participant's account earning a 10% return **Source:** Pension Dynamics, Lafayette, Calif.

smaller plans get hit with higher fees to compensate for fewer assets. Smaller firms also tend to be less sophisticated negotiators. So they may more readily accept lousy terms. Giant insurers hold 33% of small-company plan assets. Their favorite investment offering is the group variable annuity, which essentially is a family of tax-deferred mutual funds. Since all earnings in 401(k)s are already tax deferred, investing your 401(k) money in an annuity seems foolish. Some insurers, like Principal Financial, offer low-cost 401(k) plans. But most, including Cigna and Great-West, slam 401(k) participants with so-called annuity fees that average around 1.25% on top of regular administrative and investment expenses. Insurers say that covers the cost of offering flexible payouts at retirement, among other things. Dan Maul of Retirement Planning Associates, an investment advisory firm in Kirkland, Wash., disagrees. "There is no way some of these insurance company 401(k)s can justify their costs," he says.

Also feeding on the small-company market are fund families, such as American Century and Warburg Pincus, that have introduced new classes of shares of their most popular funds. These new share classes are designed to be sold by benefits firms that administer small 401(k) plans. What distinguishes the new shares from the fund's ordinary shares? The answer is additional fees, and not much else. If you purchased Warburg Pincus Growth & Income in a 401(k) managed by one of these small-plan administrators, you would have to pay investment fees equal to 1.59% of assets, nearly four-tenths of a percentage point more than if you bought the fund normally. Says Warburg Pincus managing director Gene Podsiadlo: "This is a version of a price subsidy for the employer." In other words, your boss saves at your expense.

Popular stock funds can be pricey. The trend of offering well-known funds in 401(k) plans has produced mixed results. In 1994, mutual fund companies overtook insurers as the leading providers. About 80% of the fund money is invested in branded portfolios that are also available to the public. They are called retail funds in industry jargon. Retail fund expense ratios are roughly half a percentage point higher than on institutional portfolios, where high balances lead to low costs. "Most funds used in 401(k) plans are priced two-thirds too high," says Don Phillips of fund ranker Morningstar. The growing use of retail funds has helped plan providers pump up the fees charged for every $10,000 in 401(k) assets from $51 in 1993 to $65 last year.

Many of the large employers that have signed up retail funds do not need them, let alone their high fees. Big companies have 401(k) plans with more than $300 million in assets, which is all you need to attract proven investment outfits that charge 30% to 50% less than retail fund companies. Even so, more than half of America's largest firms include retail funds in their plans. "Retail funds give our employees confidence to invest, since they know the brand names," says John Glotzbach, a retirement savings manager at Chrysler, whose 401(k) includes funds from Merrill Lynch and others. Would workers maintain their confidence in their 401(k) if they realized they are paying up to 0.5% extra a year for the convenience of looking up their fund's recent return in the newspaper? Says Mary Barneby of the National Defined Contribution Council, a plan-provider trade group: "I think a lot of employees and large employers would be floored if they understood the costs of retail funds."

Price shifting by employers is rising. A 1996 survey by Access Research found that when plan sponsors were asked to name the most important criteria in choosing a full-service 401(k) provider, cost did not even make the top 10. Instead, financial stability and reliable record keeping were the leading concerns. "About 85% to 95% of the sponsors I talk to don't know the total costs of their plans," says Joseph Valletta, a principal at HR Investments, a 401(k) plan consulting firm. "At best, they only know the administrative fees."

As a result, price competition among 401(k) providers often consists of shifting fees onto the workers by reducing the employer's administrative fees and raising the investment fees. On average, according to Access Research, the provider's administrative fee covers only 65% of its actual administrative costs. No problem. The providers more than recover by sticking their hands deeper into the workers' investment assets. Says Vanguard executive William McNabb: "The trend among providers bidding for Fortune 500 company plans is to charge minimal or even zero administrative fees." That means some employees pay all the 401(k) costs. Not surprisingly, as administrative expenses have shriveled over the past five years, total investment fees have grown 28% annually.

The 401(k) providers have a further incentive to trade administrative fees, which are based on the number of participants, for investment fees, based on plan assets. Experts say 401(k) assets are growing nine times faster than the country's work force. Thanks to the runaway bull market, company matching funds and diligent saving by workers nearing retirement, the average 401(k) participant's account grew from $20,500 to $32,010 in the past five years.

Your 401(k) costs are hard to sort out. For example, administrative and investment fees may be lumped together, making it impossible to separate the charges. Don't expect much help from the government, either. Thanks to ERISA's minimal disclosure requirements, the only document that your sponsor must send you automatically is a summary annual report, which lists the plan's total gains and losses as well as the administrative expenses. The summary annual report tells you nothing about how much you have paid in investment fees. Employers can reveal more information if they choose. But many volunteer little or nothing about costs. Take General Motors, which offers both institutional and retail Fidelity funds to employees. If you choose the institutional funds, GM pays all investment fees. But if you choose the brand-name funds, you pay. From the employees' point of view, the institutional funds enjoy a 0.5% or more head start in performance. Do employees understand that? When Money asked William Cowell, a GM benefits manager, he first ducked our question by saying: "The expenses are listed in the prospectuses." But when we pressed him, he conceded: "I'd say it's fifty-fifty."

Lobby hard for plan improvements. You can't afford to ignore high expenses and neither can the people who sign your paycheck. By law your employer is a fiduciary of the plan. That means your company has an obligation to offer as good a plan as reasonably possible. Indeed, plan sponsors have voiced concern that they may be sued in the future by employees who fail to amass enough money in their 401(k)s to fund a comfortable retirement. So chances are your company will at least consider your complaints.

To get the ball rolling, write your benefits department and explain exactly how you would like to see your plan improved. For instance, if you don't know how much your 401(k) is costing you, ask your benefits officer to explain exactly what the fees are. If you aren't happy with the answers, suggest hiring a benefits consultant to compare the costs and the options in your plan with others on the market. If you aren't supplied with information about your privately managed account, ask for detailed reports like those that retail funds distribute. If the plan provider will not cooperate, urge your company to find another one. With all the competition in the 401(k) market, companies can get plans that will keep employees informed about their investments and costs. It may also help to enlist the support of high-ranked executives, who probably have even more money in the 401(k) plan than you do. For added ammunition, identify the bottom-line advantages to the changes you would like. For example, if your company saddles employees with the plan's administrative fees, you should point out that those costs are tax deductible for the corporation but not for plan participants.

◆ PERFECT YOUR PLAN'S INVESTMENT MIX

Of all the decisions employees face in managing their 401(k)s, investing the money often provokes the highest anxiety. But it doesn't have to. Making the most of the investment options in a 401(k) isn't that complicated. You can boil the process down to some simple steps. And you don't need to be a genius at choosing top funds. Nor do you have to develop a psychic ability to call the precise moment to get into or out of the market. As noted in Chapter 5, money manager Gary Brinson of Brinson Partners in Chicago has analyzed the roles that various factors play in determining investment returns. He found that 92% of investment results can be explained by your asset mix. That's the proportions of a portfolio you dedicate to broad investment categories like stocks, bonds and cash. Other factors that many investors view as crucial, such as the choice of specific securities and the timing of purchases and sales, accounted for only 8% of the results.

If anything, asset allocation is even more important in a 401(k) plan, which will typically include funds representing half a dozen different types of assets but with only one or two of each type. After all, even if you were to have a knack for picking the year's top small-cap fund, it wouldn't do you much good if your 401(k) plan offers only one fund in that fast-expanding group. So the key to a winning strategy is quite simple. Choose the right asset mix and stick to it. These steps will set you on the right course.

Train yourself to think long term. This may be the hardest part of the whole process. To be a true long-term investor, you have to ignore the constant chattering in the business news about which funds are hot and whether the market will be up or down next week or next month. You also have to ignore the occasional visceral urge to run for the hills when the market takes a nosedive. That's harder. But it's part of the job description too. The longer your time horizon, the stronger the case for investing in your plan's stock funds, which is where you'll get the best returns. Since 1926, large-company stocks have returned almost 11% annually, double the 5.2% earned annually by intermediate-term government bonds, according to Ibbotson Associates. The problem is that stocks are much more nerve-racking than bonds in the short run. In 1974, large-company stocks' worst year of the past three decades, they lost a sickening 27% of their value. Intermediate-term bonds lost only 5% in their worst year, 1994.

The thing to remember is that a single year's loss doesn't matter much if you are looking ahead 10 years or more. You'll have ample opportunity to make up for it. If you're drawing closer than 10 years to retirement, don't confuse the end of your career with the end of your investing horizon. You will need your money to keep growing well beyond your retirement date, perhaps up to your death. Consider that the life expectancy of the typical 55-year-old woman today is more than 82 years. That means a portion of her cash must last at least 27 years. By any measure, 27 years is long-term investing.

Be honest about your stomach for risk. It's one thing to understand the theory that most investors should keep their 401(k)s primarily in stock funds for long-term growth. It's quite another to act on that theory when the market is in free-fall and your nest egg is shrinking 10% or 20% before your eyes. So level with yourself regardless of how far off your retirement may be. If you lie awake nights when stock prices dive, don't put as much of your money into stock funds as your time frame alone might suggest. Instead, you should cushion your portfolio with a larger helping of bonds. But beware of the trap of investing too conservatively. You may be overlooking the painful bite of inflation. An investor who put $1,000 in a safe money-market fund 70 years ago would have an account worth only $1,500 today after inflation is taken into account. By contrast, that same $1,000 invested in U.S. large-company stocks would have grown to about $129,800 today.

Assemble your ideal mix of investments. We asked the Vanguard Group, which manages about $60 billion in 401(k) assets, to design three model portfolios for people with varying time horizons and risk tolerances. You'll find them explained in "Smart Ways to Invest Your Stash" on the next page. If none is a perfect fit, pick the one that's closest to your age and customize it. Consider the portfolio designed for a typical 25-year-old. Some people in that age group may well conclude that the portfolio's historic return of nearly 12% a year over the past 25 years isn't worth the chance of repeating a loss of 28% in a single year. They might decide instead on a blend of 80% stocks and 20% bonds. That portfolio's worst yearly loss was a more bearable 22%.

Your employer may offer a sort of prefab portfolio that's called an asset allocation, or a lifestyle fund. About 9% of plans now have one, up from less than 1% two years ago. Lifestyle funds follow a preset asset mix aimed at a particular stage in a person's life. One that's designed for younger investors (who have a long time horizon) might hold a steady 80% stock, 20% bond mix, while one for middle-aged investors might be 60% in stocks and 40% in bonds. If your employer offers this option, we recommend that you don't go for it. The problem with one-size-fits-all is that you tend to get a bad fit. You'll do better to tailor your 401(k) to one of our recommended mixes or to a portfolio of your own devising.

Parlay your plan's strongest offerings. Once you've
decided on an overall mix, check out the specific choices your employer offers. In a typical plan, your choices include stock and bond funds, your company's own stock, a money-market fund and a so-called stable value account sponsored by a bank or insurance company. Your 401(k) plan may not offer every type of fund you see in our model portfolios. But it could someday soon. About 46% of plans now have an international or global stock fund, up from a mere 14% two years ago. In the meantime, substitute the closest available option. Here's how the 45-year-old model portfolio could be divvied up.

If your plan doesn't offer a large-company fund, find out which one most closely fills the bill by asking about what's called median market capitalization. Market cap is determined by multiplying a company's stock price by the number of shares outstanding. For a fund that buys mostly large-company stocks, the answer should be $5 billion or more. If that question proves too difficult for your benefits department, ask about the fund's 10 largest stockholdings. A host of familiar names such as Eastman Kodak, IBM, Johnson & Johnson, Philip Morris and General Electric is an

These three model portfolios were designed for 401(k) investors at distinctly different stages of their careers. One of them may fit you right off the rack. Or you may want to tailor the closest one to better fit your age and risk tolerance. If you're risk-shy, you can lighten up on stocks and put more money into bond funds instead. For each portfolio, we show annual returns for a recent 25-year period as well as the best and worst years for the allocations.

For 25–year–olds, an aggressive mix
[100% stocks]

Annual return	Best year (1980)	Worst year (1974)
12%	35%	−28%

■ Large-company stock funds
■ Small-company stock funds
■ International stock funds

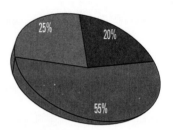

For 45–year–olds, a moderate blend
[80% stocks, 20% bonds]

Annual return	Best year (1975)	Worst year (1974)
11%	31%	−22%

■ Large-company stock funds
■ Small-company stock funds
■ International stock funds
□ Intermediate bond funds

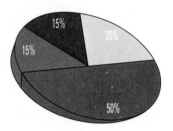

For 55–year–olds, a less risky recipe
[60% stocks, 40% bonds]

Annual return	Best year (1975)	Worst year (1974)
10%	28%	−18%

■ Large-company stock funds
■ Small-company stock funds
■ International stock funds
□ Intermediate bond funds

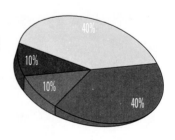

Sources: The Vanguard Group, Lipper Analytical Services

indication that the fund favors large companies. Other tip-offs are funds labeled blue chip, growth and income or S&P 500 index. One word of warning. No matter how much you like the company you work for, don't bet your retirement on its stock. Experts say the absolute maximum you should invest in any single stock is 10%. If you find you have more company stock than that, ask your plan administrator whether you can move the excess into a more diversified stock fund. If anybody asks, you aren't being disloyal, just prudent.

If your plan doesn't have a small-company fund, look for one with a median market cap of $1 billion or less. Funds labeled aggressive growth often hold a healthy share of small stocks. If your plan doesn't offer such a fund, stick this slice of your portfolio into a large-company fund instead. Ditto if your 401(k) offers no funds with international or global in their names. If your plan doesn't have an intermediate-term bond fund, a general bond fund that holds issues of all maturities, from one to 30 years, would be the next best thing. If your plan lacks any kind of bond fund, a stable value account would be a fair substitute. Stable value accounts typically consist of contracts, issued by insurance companies or banks, that promise to pay a set rate of interest for a certain period, often two to five years. The accounts usually offer higher yields than money-market funds by one percentage point or more a year. Before you invest in one, however, check that it's diversified among at least five different issuers or otherwise protected against the risk of default. If you have none of those options, you probably should use a money-market fund.

*Redeploy your investments periodically.*Check your

401(k) portfolio once or twice a year and, if necessary, bring it back into line with the asset mix you've chosen. If stocks rose, say, 30% in value over the past year while bonds went up only 10%, you'll find that you have more in stock funds and less in bond funds than your model portfolio calls for. To keep things in balance, shift money out of the stock account and into bonds. That said, don't fall prey to the impulse to change investments willy-nilly. Trying to time the market by jumping from stocks to bonds or vice versa at the right moment is a game most pros lose. A good mix of assets will prosper over the long term. But it won't guarantee great returns every month along the way. So strive to ride through the bad patches, keeping your eye on your long-term goal of a prosperous retirement.

◆ TAP A 401(K) WHILE YOU'RE WORKING

It's fairly easy to get your hands on your 401(k) funds if you understand the rules. For example, you can withdraw money from your account while you're working only if you're suffering a financial hardship. Yet you can always borrow against your account if your company allows loans. In fact, at any given time 20% of 401(k) participants are borrowing against their plans. Once you're retired and older than 59.5, you can take money out of your plan without owing tax penalties. Taking money out, however, makes sense only if you're very careful and really need to do so. After all, extracting money from your 401(k) means thumbing your nose at an immediate tax shelter, siphoning off your retirement savings, possibly forgoing investment earnings plus perhaps boosting your current tax bill. Still, pulling money out sometimes can be a handy way to help reach other financial goals. Read on to learn more about how best to withdraw your 401(k) money and when alternative sources of cash are smarter.

Deft ways to take money out. Promise yourself that you won't succumb to temptation and pull money out of your 401(k) just to have more spare cash on hand. But you may have a legitimate reason such as buying a new home to take money out of your account. There are two options–loans and hardship withdrawals. Roughly 80% of companies with 401(k) plans now let employees borrow as much as half the money in their accounts to a maximum of $50,000. If your company permits it, you can even have more than one loan going at the same time as long as your outstanding debt does not exceed the limits. Some employers allow loans only for serious purposes, such as buying or remodeling a home. But nine out of 10 plans that allow loans let you borrow for any reason at all.

Borrowing is much smarter than withdrawing cash. With a loan you eventually replace the money in your own tax-sheltered account. You have five years to repay the loan or, if you're using the money to buy a home, as long as 30 years. Loans let you avoid owing the immediate taxes due on withdrawals and the 10% penalty for nonretired people younger than 59.5. A 401(k) loan also tends to be one of the least expensive ways to borrow today. The interest rate is generally one or two percentage points above the prime lending rate. By contrast, banks typically charge six or more points over prime for personal loans.

There are two major drawbacks to such a loan. First, borrowed 401(k) money earns only the interest you pay yourself, not the higher returns the cash might earn if you had kept it invested in the plan. The other problem is that to keep a loan you normally must keep your job. Fewer than a third of employers with 401(k) loan provisions let former workers continue making installment payments. If you quit or get laid off, you may have to pay off the entire loan within three months. If you default on the loan, the IRS will treat the unpaid balance as a withdrawal that's subject to income taxes and a 10% penalty if you're under age 59.5 and haven't retired. A large unpaid 401(k) loan balance could even push you into a higher tax bracket.

Given these risks, homeowners needing cash for important expenses like college or medical emergencies ought to consider a home-equity loan instead. With a home-equity loan, your interest rate won't be much higher than the going rate charged by your company's 401(k). And unlike a 401(k) loan, interest on a home-equity loan is usually tax deductible. As a result, your money is almost certain to earn more if left in the plan than it will cost you, after tax, to borrow against your home. Say you're in the 28% federal tax bracket and you pay 5% in state and local taxes. A 9.7% home-equity loan costs you just 6.5% after your deduction. You should be earning more than that on your 401(k) investments.

Make sure to remix your portfolio. Also remember that by taking out a fixed-rate loan on which you pay interest to yourself, you're effectively adding a fixed-income investment to your 401(k) account. You may therefore need to remix your plan's portfolio to make up for the low return on the loan. Ask your benefits department how the company will debit the loan. Some employers deduct it from your least speculative investments. But it's more commonly drawn proportionately from all the funds in your account. Then, if necessary, adjust your portfolio to keep the investment mix on track with your goals and risk tolerance. Here's an example. Say you have a $20,000 account balance that's 50% invested in a stock fund, 25% in a bond fund and 25% in a guaranteed investment contract (GIC). You want to borrow $5,000 drawn from the funds. To keep the same investment mix, you should put two-thirds of the remaining GIC balance, or $2,500, in the stock fund and the other third, or $1,250, in the bond fund. That way you again have $10,000 in the stock fund, $5,000 in the bond fund and $5,000 in a fixed-income investment.

Let's say that a financial emergency strikes, and you need cash. But you have maxed out on borrowing, or your employer doesn't offer loans. Fortunately, 92% of employers with 401(k)s permit early withdrawals for financial hardship. Most stick to four hardship exemptions cited in the tax code. The four are paying college tuition for yourself or a dependent; purchasing your primary residence; covering any out-of-pocket medical costs; and preventing foreclosure or eviction from your primary residence. Some 18% of plans permit other types of hardship withdrawals such as for funeral expenses or child support.

The real cost of tapping your account. The ability to withdraw money from your 401(k) provides a comforting safety net. But it's a pricey option that should be used only as a last resort. Keep in mind that this is an irreversible move. You can't replace the money later on. What's more, you'll owe income taxes on the amount you take out of the 401(k) and probably the 10% penalty for early withdrawal. Worst of all, by law your employer must withhold 20% up front for taxes. To receive the money you really need, you have to take out 25% more than you want. When you file your tax return, you'll get credit for the 20% you paid. But you'll have to ante up any additional taxes that are due. To get your hands on an immediate $10,000, for example, you would need to withdraw $12,500. Next April, if you're in the 28% federal income tax bracket and pay 5% in state and local taxes, you would owe an additional $1,000 in taxes plus a 10% penalty of $1,250. And don't overlook about $625 in state and local taxes. So the amount you'd ultimately keep from a $12,500 withdrawal would be just $7,125, or 57% of what you took out of your plan. (The withdrawal penalties are waived if you are 55 or over and have retired early.)

Rather than forcing your employer to act as a private investigator and prove that you have no other source for the money, the IRS okays hardship withdrawals as long as your company prohibits you from contributing to your 401(k) for a year after making a withdrawal. As a result, during that time, you forgo not just your tax-sheltered salary deduction but also any employer match as well. Given all these drawbacks, if a cash crunch hits, you'd probably be better off dipping into your emergency funds or getting a loan from your family and friends.

The moves to make when you change jobs. Resist the temptation to make the most common 401(k) mistake of taking your entire account in cash rather than reinvesting it in another tax-deferred plan. (Other major mistakes are having too much money parked in cash or socked in your company's stock.) A whopping 79% of workers who quit or get fired and take the cash from their 401(k) plans elect not to reinvest all of it in another plan. By failing to do so, you subject your savings to immediate taxes and the 10% penalty for withdrawals. You also jeopardize your future financial security because compounding tax-deferred money is the best way to save for retirement.

If possible, when you leave a job and a 401(k), choose instead one of the three options. You can leave your money where it is, transfer it to your new employer's 401(k) plan or roll it into an IRA. As long as your account exceeds $3,500, you can leave your money in your former employer's plan until you retire. You won't be able to contribute more to it. But the account will keep making money for you, and you can always roll over the money into a different sheltered account later. So if you need time to think over your options, this might be the best short-term move. Long term, however, there are disadvantages to leaving the money in your former employer's 401(k). For starters, you won't be allowed to borrow against the account. And since you can no longer contribute to it, the company won't match any funds. So unless the investments in your account are doing spectacularly well, don't leave your money in your old plan any longer than necessary.

If your new employer offers a 401(k), you usually can transfer your cash to that plan. You may have to wait a year or so to become eligible to make new contributions, however. Switching from one employer's plan to another is your best strategy because a 401(k) and its cousins at non-profits are the only savings program that offer matching contributions. If you roll money into a new 401(k), however, make sure your old employer hands over the money to the new plan's trustee, not to you. If you are the recipient, your employer has to withhold 20% for taxes. What's more, you'll have to replace the missing 20% from your own pocket within the 60 days allowed for a rollover. Otherwise, that amount will be considered a withdrawal, subject to taxes and the 10% penalty.

An IRA is your best bet if your new company has no 401(k) plan or doesn't allow rollovers. One tip is to set up a new IRA account, sometimes called a conduit IRA, and then keep your mitts off it. If you don't mix that money with other contributions, you'll be allowed to roll it back into a 401(k) plan in the future. As with the transfer described above, make sure the money goes directly to your IRA trustee.

◆ WITHDRAWING MONEY IN RETIREMENT

Congratulations certainly are in order. You've made it to age 59.5, the stage in your career in which you finally can kiss those rules regarding 401(k) early withdrawals and tax penalties good-bye. You've worked hard, endeavored to invest wisely, kept borrowing to a minimum and are ready to start enjoying the fruits of your labor in retirement.

Not so fast. When it's time to start pulling money out of your 401(k), you'll face a tangle of irrevocable tax and investment decisions that could tarnish your golden years if you mishandle them. Make the right moves, however, and your 401(k) will be your ticket to a cushy retirement. Your first step is to hire a professional tax adviser. Says Paul Westbrook, a retirement planner in Ridgewood, N.J.: "Deciding how to handle your 401(k) at retirement is not a do-it-yourself job." To help guide you, we've laid out the most common questions about 401(k) withdrawals in retirement and the wisest answers, according to financial planners and benefits consultants.

◆ When do I have to start taking money out of my 401(k)?

The law says you can begin making penalty-free withdrawals at 59.5, or 55 if you took early retirement. But you don't have to begin shoveling out any of the cash until you are 70.5. If you can swing it, try to draw on funds outside your 401(k) and other tax-favored accounts, letting you continue to shelter your earnings from the IRS for as long as possible.

◆ What if my 401(k) is thriving, and my former employer will let me leave the money where it is?

You probably should do just that. For one thing, this will give you even more time to map out your post-career investment strategy. "A lot of investment sharks are after this money," warns Harry Purnell, an actuary at the benefits firm Foster Higgins based in Princeton, N.J. Equally important, leaving the money in the 401(k) may offer you tax advantages that the alternative, a rollover IRA, can't match. Since the tax law limits annual pretax contributions to 401(k) plans to $9,500, some companies allow employees to contribute after-tax dollars as well. The hitch? The law won't let you invest after-tax money in a rollover IRA when you retire. So if your 401(k) fund has sizable after-tax contributions, leaving the money alone is the only way to get tax deferral on your entire account. What's more, once you transfer money to an IRA, you forgo the right to elect

HOW TO TRIM YOUR 401(K) TAX BILL

As this table shows, the best way to preserve your retirement nest egg from taxes is to roll over your payout into an IRA and let the fund continue to grow tax deferred. The worst is pocketing your 401(k) cash and paying ordinary income tax on the total. Our calculations assume that a 60-year-old couple with $40,000 of annual taxable income receive a 401(k) payout worth $300,000 that they wish to draw on until age 90. The after-tax amounts assume a 33% federal and state tax rate.

401(K) WITHDRAWAL OPTION	INITIAL TAX	NET SUM INVESTED	ANNUAL AFTER-TAX INCOME FROM 401(K) AGES 60 TO 65	ANNUAL AFTER-TAX INCOME FROM 401(K) AGES 65 TO 90
IRA rollover with no withdrawals for five years	$0	$300,000	$0	$27,666
IRA rollover with immediate withdrawals	0	300,000	17,854	17,854
Lump sum with 10-year averaging	81,330	218,670	14,813	14,813
Lump sum with five-year averaging	83,680	216,322	14,654	14,654
Lump sum with immediate taxation	118,640	181,360	12,286	12,286

Source: Westbrook Financial Advisers, Ridgewood, N.J. Inside the rollover IRA, the money earns a tax-deferred 8% annually. Comparable investments are made outside the IRA. But earnings on them are taxable.

the special tax treatment that could be available if you pocket a lump-sum payout. For details, see "How to Trim Your 401(k) Tax Bill" above.

Be sure to check out your plan's rules regarding retirees' accounts in its latest summary plan description. If the information isn't there, you should ask your plan administrator for a set of written rules. Some can be restrictive. Once you leave the company, for example, your 401(k) might not let you switch among the various investment options as often as you could when you were an employee. In addition, most plans won't let you take sporadic withdrawals. Instead, they require you to take out all or nothing at all.

◆ **What if my ex–employer won't let me leave my account where it is or I'd rather invest it myself?** Move the money to a rollover IRA. You can roll the money into an existing IRA or open a new one. To do this properly, instruct your 401(k) plan administrator either to transfer the money directly by wire into your IRA or to give you a check that's made out to your IRA trustee. The distribution check shouldn't be made payable to you. If it is, you have 60 days to transfer the money into an IRA account yourself. If you don't act within 60 days, the entire amount is deemed taxable. To make matters worse, if the check is made out to you, your employer must withhold 20% for income taxes. So if you have amassed a $100,000 account, you would get a check for only $80,000. To roll over the entire $100,000 within the 60-day window, you'd have to come up with the missing $20,000 on your own and add it to the $80,000 check you deposit in your IRA. Can't come up with the 20 grand? Then the tax law says you've made a taxable withdrawal of that amount. Thus you'll owe income tax on the $20,000. That's a $6,600 hit assuming a combined 33% federal, state and local tax bracket.

◆ **What are my options if I want to take my 401(k) cash now to buy the RV of my retirement dreams?** If you don't want to roll over your stash, you need to plan ahead to minimize your tax hit. The best strategy for reducing Uncle Sam's bill is to use a special calculation called forward averaging. Five-year forward averaging is available to anyone 59.5 or older who has participated in his or her 401(k) for at least five years before the year of the distribution. You compute the taxes due as if you received the money over five years instead of all at once. Without averaging, a couple getting a $300,000 lump-sum 401(k) payout might owe $118,640 in taxes, assuming they had $40,000 of other income. With five-year averaging, the tax would be $83,680, or 29% less. The benefits of five-year averaging wane as your payout gets larger. Note, however, that once your distribution tops $1,318,750, five-year averaging gives you the same tax bill as the ordinary income tax calculation.

Were you born before 1936? If so, you can instead choose 10-year forward averaging, which often saves you even more in taxes. With 10-year averaging, you compute your tax as if you had received your payout over 10 years, using the tax rates for singles that were in effect in 1986. For distributions of up to $358,250, this is the way to go if you qualify. Using this example, the tax you would owe on $300,000 with 10-year averaging would be just $81,330, vs. $83,680 using the five-year method. If you take lump-sum distributions from more than one retirement plan during the year, you must apply it to all your lumps. So if you would like to roll over one of the payouts into an IRA and forward average the other, arrange to take your distributions in different years.

Here's one final caution. If you plan to use forward averaging on a lump sum exceeding $775,000 this year, you could be hit with a 15% excise tax penalty on the amount over $775,000. This is the result of so-called excess distribution rules designed to ensure that taxpayers use 401(k)s and other tax-sheltered plans to build up an adequate retirement fund, not to amass family fortunes. The threshold is adjusted periodically for inflation. If you're planning on taking $775,000 in a lump sum, see your tax adviser before you do. He or she may be able to suggest ways to avoid or mitigate the combination of taxes and penalties that you will owe.

◆ What if I'll need some, but not all, of the cash soon?

Then you'll most likely want to dump your 401(k) into a rollover IRA and make taxable withdrawals as needed. But unless you have to, don't take out more than $155,000 in any single year. Here's why. If the sum of your annual withdrawals from all of your tax-sheltered nest eggs exceeds $155,000, you'll get nailed with a 15% penalty on the excess in addition to the income tax. The $155,000 annual limit also adjusts for inflation but increases only in $5,000 increments.

◆ Can my ex–employer give me periodic payments?

That depends on whether the company is among the roughly 33% of 401(k) plan sponsors that offer an installment payment option. If it is, you select a payout period that's typically five to 15 years. Choose 10 years, for example, and you'll get one-tenth of your balance in Year One, one-ninth in Year Two and so on until your account is finally depleted at the end of 10 years.

◆ What steps do I have to start taking at age 70.5?

At this age you must begin withdrawing specified annual amounts out of all your tax-sheltered accounts. How you make these withdrawals will have income tax consequences and possibly estate tax repercussions as well. To brush up on the rules and the issues surrounding mandatory distributions, get a copy of IRS Publication 590–Individual Retirement Arrangements. It's available free by calling 800-829-3676. The minimum amount you must withdraw once you turn 70.5 is based on two factors. The first is your life expectancy as determined by IRS tables. (If you have a beneficiary, you'll use one figure representing your joint life expectancy.) The second is the total you have in each tax-sheltered account. If you and your spouse are both 71, your joint life expectancy is 19.8 years. If you have a $100,000 rollover IRA, you must withdraw at least $5,050 ($100,000 divided by 19.8). You can take out more. But failure to take at least the required minimum means owing a tax penalty equal to a staggering 50% of the shortfall.

To lower your minimum annual payout, try to name as young a beneficiary as you can. Most people choose their spouse. But if he or she is adequately provided for through other means, naming someone younger will help both of you stretch your 401(k) money in retirement. A younger sibling raises your joint life expectancy. This in turn lowers your payout. The 71-year-old IRA owner in the above example would lower his mandatory payout from $5,050 to $3,950 if his beneficiary was 61 instead of 71. Are you suddenly feeling very generous toward your 12-year-old grandchild? Forget it. If your beneficiary is not your spouse, the IRS tables impose a maximum 10-year age spread between you and your beneficiary to prevent you from drastically reducing your payouts.

There's more red tape to tackle, of course. For example, you'll need to select a method for calculating your life expectancy. The IRS permits two methods dubbed recalculation and term certain. The choice you make is irrevocable, so consider your options carefully.

Under the recalculation method, the IRS uses an actuarial table to figure the life expectancy of you and your beneficiary every year. Based on the reassuring conviction that the longer you live, the longer you're expected to go on living, the recalculation method reduces your life expectancy by less than one year for each year that you live. This method is particularly appropriate if you want to stretch out your minimum payments over as many years as possible and maximize your tax-deferred buildup of capital.

In contrast, the term-certain option establishes your life expectancy up front and then drops it by one year every year. Thus your 401(k) account is depleted sooner than if you used the recalculation method. You may prefer this if you want to assure yourself a stream of payouts for a definite time period but are also interested in pulling money out of your account so that you can give it as a gift to your heirs. Such gifts reduce the size of your estate and possible future estate taxes.

INDEX